HAPPINESS *in the Age of*
AMBITION

Accolades and appreciation for the book

This book takes you through the life of a person with a vision and mission—Dr H.P. Kanoria.
Dr Murli Manohar Joshi, former President, Bharatiya Janata Party, and Padma Bhushan awardee

Dr Kanoria not only provided employment to people and earned wealth but also carried out many social welfare activities for his fellow countrymen.
Santosh Kumar Gangwar, Minister of State Labour & Employment (Independent Charge), Government of India

This book is the journey of a village boy who developed the largest NBFC and holistic infrastructure company in India. He is great motivation for all.
General (Dr) V.K. Singh (Retd), Minister of State for Road Transport & Highways, Government of India

This book will compel readers to become their better version.
Arjun Ram Meghwal, IAS (Retd.), Minister of State for Heavy Industries & Public Enterprises and Parliamentary Affairs, Government of India

Dr Kanoria is among the architects of modern India who has truly demonstrated '*Idam Na Mum, Idam Rashtrayay*', meaning 'It is not mine, it is for the nation'.
Ashwini Kumar Choubey, Minister of State for Health & Family Welfare, Government of India

Dr Kanoria is always active in taking up different projects to build a strong society and nation.
Giriraj Singh, Minister of Animal Husbandry, Dairying and Fisheries, Government of India

Dr Kanoria has lived a good life, a life of service and compassion.
Maneka Sanjay Gandhi, Member of Parliament

I hope this biography will inspire many.
Hukumdev Narayan Yadav, former Member of Parliament (Lok Sabha)

Dr Kanoria endures his [astute] business management with a genuine commitment to spirituality and high values—a rare combination.
Dr Karan Singh, former Member of Parliament (Rajya Sabha)

The story of Dr Hari Prasad Kanoria is a saga of a village boy with organizational abilities, vision, courage and entrepreneurship, who has been a path-breaker.
Sitaram Sharma, Hony Consul of Republic of Belarus in Kolkata, and President, Bharat Chamber of Commerce

HAPPINESS *in the Age of* AMBITION

The Story of a Corporate Spiritualist
HARI PRASAD KANORIA

by
Megha Bajaj

RUPA

Published by
Rupa Publications India Pvt. Ltd 2020
7/16, Ansari Road, Daryaganj
New Delhi 110002

Sales Centres:
Allahabad Bengaluru Chennai
Hyderabad Jaipur Kathmandu
Kolkata Mumbai

Copyright © Kanoria Foundation and Megha Bajaj 2020

Photographs courtesy: Kanoria Foundation

The views and opinions expressed in this book are the author's own and the facts are as reported by her which have been verified to the extent possible, and the publishers are not in any way liable for the same.

All rights reserved.
No part of this publication may be reproduced, transmitted, or stored in a retrieval system, in any form or by any means, electronic, mechanical, photocopying, recording or otherwise, without the prior permission of the publisher.

ISBN: 978-93-5333-849-7

First impression 2020

10 9 8 7 6 5 4 3 2 1

Printed at Replika Press Pvt. Ltd, India.

The moral right of the author has been asserted.

This book is sold subject to the condition that it shall not, by way of trade or otherwise, be lent, resold, hired out, or otherwise circulated, without the publisher's prior consent, in any form of binding or cover other than that in which it is published.

Contents

Foreword — vii
Preface — ix

1. The Beginnings — 1
2. Days of Innocence — 5
3. Seeds of Spirituality — 8
4. Much Like a Tree — 10
5. Why Waste? — 12
6. Walking the Thin Line — 14
7. Bullying the Bully — 16
8. Go Green — 18
9. The Power of Prayer — 20
10. Ma to Ma Kali — 22
11. The End of an Era — 24
12. Swami and Me — 26
13. All For One and One For All — 30
14. Fat to Fit — 32
15. *Carpe Diem!* — 34
16. The Right Word — 36
17. The Rebel — 38
18. Get It Done! — 40
19. Sweet Money — 42
20. A Book in Time — 43
21. The Joy of Small Things — 45
22. My Friend Sancheti — 47
23. The Circle of Life — 49
24. A Partnership for Life — 52
25. Breaking Norms — 54
26. Brain and Sandesh — 56
27. What's in a Name? — 57
28. The Fine Balance — 61
29. Education Unfolds Potential — 64
30. Let Them Fight — 66

31. Bande Mataram and Rasgulla	68
32. Do Not Invite Me	71
33. Face the Brutes	74
34. Me' vs 'We'	78
35. The Uprising	81
36. Your Company is Too Small	84
37. Small Will Become Big	88
38. Faith in Self; Faith in God	90
39. Wedding Bells	92
40. Return on Investment	99
41. Vishnu Loka	104
42. Taking Wings	106
43. What More, What Next?	109
44. The Power of Pen	111
45. Of Failures and Learnings	114
46. Turning Information into Opportunity	116
47. Are You Ready for the Risk?	118
48. The Way Forward	120
49. The Strength of a Grass	122
50. Surviving the Storm	124
51. When Life Hands You Lemons…	126
52. Adventures and Misadventures	130
53. Food for Soul	132
54. A Help in Time…	134
55. Lessons in Divinity	136
56. Reliving the Past	139
57. The Little Guru	141
58. Strong Roots, Powerful Wings	143
59. The Great Wall of China	146
60. Giving Back	149
61. The Survivors	151
62. The Power of Faith	153
63. The Spiritual Confluence	155
64. My Friend Kalam	164
65. A Child at Heart	167
66. Paradox No More	170

Foreword

I am immensely elated to know that a biography focusing on the life and work of Dr H.P. Kanoria titled *Happiness in the Age of Ambition: The Story of a Corporate Spiritualist* is being published.

Dr Kanoria is a business tycoon with a difference. A Presidencian of the Economics Department of the Presidency College, Dr Kanoria could have been a great economist of repute, but he chose to be an industrialist. This was not because he wanted to build a huge fortune for himself but because he wanted to serve his country, indeed his Mother, by providing shelter to as many of her children as possible. By the grace of the Mother that happened much to his satisfaction.

His main contribution to the business world is establishing SREI, the largest NBFC in India. His guiding principle—work with devotion and righteousness—has helped in taking his business to its current high.

His business network has spread all over the country now and is being looked after successfully by his able children. Dr Kanoria is now supremely happy involving himself in exploring the mystery of the inner life. I am happy for my association with this ardent devotee of the Divine who is now least bothered about his business but very much concerned instead with the future of humanity. He is receiving unstinting support from his family to continue his charity work; hold seminars, programmes of immense proportions; publish books on values and so on.

From his articles and books and devotional service it is obvious that his only desire is to infuse among the people the lofty ideal of seeking the dignity of man and thus build a civil society everywhere.

He has been constantly working for promoting education, especially among the weaker section of the society and women empowerment through several initiatives like the Institute for Inspiration and Self-Development, Acid Survivors and Women Welfare Foundation and Srihari Global School. In addition to numerous national awards, he has received international recognition for his outstanding service at the Global Officials of Dignity (GOD) Awards at the United Nations, New York.

Fighting against so many odds he has reached the summit of success in the corporate world. But the spiritual flavor of his life has made his career unique in the sense that his life conveys the valued message to the society that sheer material progress without spiritual development is hollow and worthless.

I pray that his life will be beacon light of hope and inspiration to the coming generations.

Swami Suparnananda
Secretary, The Ramakrishna Mission Institute of Culture,
Kolkata

Preface

'The answers that you seek are seeking you…'

I woke up, startled. Was someone speaking to me, or was it just my imagination? I was tempted to pinch myself to make sure that I was not dreaming. And yet a part of me did not want to wake up, for I had been waiting so long to hear these words.

Once again, a voice within me whispered, 'The answers that you seek are seeking you…'

I have always believed that life has an answer to every question. However, one can never tell when the answers will reveal themselves. I believe one needs to go through certain experiences to understand the answers that life unfolds. Only then does that mystical connection of dots happen. Else, one may just lose these priceless pearls of wisdom—a zillion nuggets of wisdom, like the sparkling stars in inky skies. And the question—which one is yours, which one will change your life forever—remains a mystery eternally.

For the longest time I had wondered, how can one lead a fulfilling life? Do the answers lie in spirituality or in materialism? A seeker at heart, I was drawn to meditation from a very young age. Love, surrender and faith were words/ideas that I wanted to experience as the truth of my own life. I read my first spiritual text at the tender age of 16, sitting atop a rusty water tank on my terrace, facing the sea, on Napean Sea Road. An idealist at heart and innocent in my way of thinking, I trudged along, hoping that I would find in spirituality all that I had been looking for.

As I grew older, the confusion began. While my soul sought solitude, I realized that to survive in this world, I needed people skills. I was not a hermit having an isolated existence in some craggy cave in the Himalayas. I was a young girl who had to go to school, college, find her passion—all of this required relationship skills, people skills, and tact, something I inherently lacked.

Furthermore, as I entered the professional world, I started to realize the importance of financial prudence, of knowing how to deal with cut-throat competition, working hard and working smart.

Somehow my sadhana (routine spiritual practice) and spiritual quest always seemed to be at loggerheads with the ways of the world. So much so that I started feeling that I could either pursue spirituality or become a part of the world of materialism. Both were not possible.

Whenever I saw someone very successful in life, I wondered if they were also spiritual at heart. Had they reached the pinnacle of their career while remaining grounded in the divine? Similarly, every time I saw a spiritually enlightened soul I wondered, were they not losing out on the abundance of material life—the delights of food, travel and luxuries? Had they truly been able to resist the temptations, or was it just a facade? I never could make out. Unfortunately, reading about industrialists committing suicides at the peak of their careers or gurus/godmen getting embroiled in scandals didn't help my case—it furthered my confusion.

Once again the voice within echoed in the chambers of my heart, 'The answers that you seek are seeking you…'

Finally, the day arrived when I was scheduled to travel to Kolkata to meet Hari Prasad Kanoria, a billionaire in his late seventies and the founder, trustee and chairman of Kanoria Foundation, SREI and several other companies. Did he have answers to some of my questions? Was something within me about to unravel at last?

I didn't know what to expect.

After all, I had met him only once. Every year he organized a conference—the World Confluence of Humanity, Power & Spirituality—and on one occasion I was invited as the youngest speaker.

Clad in a black suit, with numerous brooches advocating patriotism, unity among religions, women's welfare and whatnot, Hari Prasad appeared to be a man of vision and purpose. And yet, as his round countenance broke into a smile, he seemed just like a child. I admired the way he demonstrated both age-old wisdom and child-like innocence and felt drawn to his enigmatic personality. So, when his beautiful daughter, Manisha, who happens to be a soul friend of mine, contacted me, asking me to write his biography, I was excited. I however took six months to respond with a yes, and I was grateful for her patience and trust in my words.

It would be interesting to meet him again. I was sure of that. But would he really have answers to the questions that had been haunting me for so many years? I wasn't sure.

It is in this state of mind—looking forward and yet not knowing what to expect—that I boarded the 5.05 a.m. Jet Airways flight from Mumbai to Kolkata without any inkling that my life was about to change. And how!

During my interview sessions with Hari Prasad Kanoria, I gradually realized that there were many key attributes that had contributed to the making of the legend he was.

Read this book like a story. Don't rush through it. It is meant to be savoured like a delicately cooked appetizer—bit by bit. Allow yourself the time to ponder. To wonder. To ruminate. And most importantly, get inspired!

Chapter 1

The Beginnings

Imagine a small village with skies as blue as the crayons with green grass that sways gently now and stands still just a little later, caressed by the wind. A land situated along the Gangetic belt, with fertile soil and the fragrance of wet earth as its very essence.

It was in a little village called Barhiya in Bihar, that a baby boy was born nearly eight decades ago. The cosmos chose a good day for this round-faced, gurgling bundle of joy to come into existence.

His great grandfather, Raghunath Roy, and grandfather had built a palatial house in the centre of the village's market area in 1800 or so. His father, Kedarnath, was born in 1920. He was born on 11 January 1942. Due to the family's belief and for religious reasons Hari Prasad's birthday is celebrated on 31 December.

His birth marked the beginning of a new era for the Kanoria family. To be the firstborn of Kedarnath and Bhagirathi Devi was no trivial affair. The elated grandparents, Hanumandas, and Banarasi Devi, who were known in the village first for their benevolence and then for their affluence, celebrated the event by doing what they did best: giving.

Love, laughter, money, gifts and sweets were shared in abundance even as the baby, named Hari Prasad, remained unaware of all the wheels of happiness that his birth had turned. So not just the Kanoria household, the entire village rejoiced at the arrival of the little one. In fact, on the day of his birth there was not a single villager who went to sleep on an empty stomach.

Hari, as he was lovingly called by all, was born in a family with a rich heritage. His forefathers hailed from Khurana Kanore, located some twenty km away from Mahendragarh (formerly in Rajasthan, now in Haryana). They traversed a thousand km-long journey across the desert, braving hardships with courage, enterprise and an instinct for risk-taking before settling in the eastern part of the country—in Barhiya (Bihar) and Calcutta.

The Kanoria family was engaged in the trading of foodgrains, pulses and lentils and agri-products and moneylending. The family's business was spread across the country—from Lahore in Punjab in pre-Partition India to Madras (now Chennai) in the southern part of the country.

Their home, Laxmikunj, was nothing short of a landmark in the village. Anyone seeking directions to a place in Barhiya near the Kanoria haveli, was invariably told to look out for the large fortress-like haveli as a landmark. To have a palatial house—with a spacious courtyard, twenty rooms and four kitchens—housing thirty members across three generations, was no mean feat.

The Kanoria house had a beautiful temple on the premises. One would naturally assume that this was meant only for family members, but the remarkable thing about the Kanoria family, boundless in generosity, was that they had thrown open the temple gates to everybody. Anyone could come to the sanctum to pray, to feel one with their God. The walls of the Kanoria home were not built on the foundation of discrimination—making a difference in people's lives was as natural as breathing for them.

The village where Hari was born had very fertile land as it was located on the Gangetic belt. The land in and around the village was flooded every year, with the receding water depositing fertile silt on it. Big, small and marginal farmers would come to sell their produce—especially horse gram and lentils of all varieties (red masoor, arhar, kesari). Marginal farmers would bring three to four bags of produce (each bag weighing fifty kg) on ponies. Naughty little Hari would have a field day having fun rides while his grandfather was engaged in various business dealings.

Hanumandas had a large automatic pulses packing machine. Both the house and the unit had their own power house for generating electricity. The family had at home many cows and a few horses. They also had Victorian and other carriers, and even an Austin car.

Hari grew up observing his grandfather act not only as the head of the family but also the village. Each day was like a 'mela' in the Kanoria home. Villagers would come to Hari's grandfather not just with their produce but also with their worries and challenges, only to be soothed with food and words of wisdom which helped them tackle most of their day-to-day issues.

It is believed that the right start to a journey leads to the right destination. In the case of Hari, this statement was absolutely true, for his upbringing played a key role in bestowing on him the qualities that would be of great value in the latter years of his life. The first quality, needless to say, was benevolence.

As I listened to Hari Prasad reliving his childhood days, sometimes with a gentle smile, at other times with moist eyes, I realized that not all of us are as blessed as he was—to be born with a silver spoon in his mouth—and have people dote on our very existence. And yet, while the right upbringing may not be in our hands, to gift ourselves the right qualities certainly is in our hands. Some are born to it; others may need to cultivate those qualities. Either way it is possible.

As Hari Prasad unveiled his life one chapter at a time, some left me speechless, and others made me want to immediately scream out from the rooftop that I had gained certain life-changing insights. I realized just how important each of these attributes had been in the shaping of the towering personality before me.

The house where two generations of the Kanorias, both Kedarnath, Hari's father, and Hari were born. It was built during 1880-1881

The house was built by Hari's grandfather in 1950. Hari, who was a young boy at the time, learnt everything about construction when this was being built.

Chapter 2

Days of Innocence

Hari was nine years old when he began his life in the beautiful village of Barhiya. Hari's father, Kedarnath, had completed his schooling in the village and then studied in Presidency College, Calcutta. When he was six months old, Hari and his mother went to Calcutta to join Kedarnath at 150, Vivekananda Road (near the birthplace of Swami Vivekananda).

After Gurupathshala, he was admitted to the Maheshwari School in Burrabazar, Calcutta. During the rainy season, the road always got flooded. Putting their books under their shirts, Hari and his friends would walk in the dirty rainwater which came up to their knees. It was great fun for them.

The Gurupathshala was located right next to a Ram temple. There was a very strict master who would roam around with a thin stick in his hand. A whack here, a thwack there—learning was as much about the alphabet and numbers as it was about shouting and punishments. The teacher had the habit of punishing the children by telling them, 'Murga bano' (The word 'murga' means rooster in Hindi. The punishment involves takes a position like that of a rooster, squatting and then looping the arms behind the knees to firmly hold the ears.) The memory of this punishment was so deep seated that decades later, Hari used it to create an atmosphere of fun and laughter in his office by often asking the staff to become a 'murga' as an atonement for petty mistakes!

When he was a little older it was decided that he would be sent back to Barhiya. His grandparents doted on him and wished to bring up the child themselves. After returning to the village, he was admitted to the village high school, which was at a walking distance from the Kanoria home.

The love and pampering that the grandparents bestowed on Hari sure had its impact on him. He was an extremely happy and fearless child, roaming freely through the village—plucking flowers, rolling in the meadows, drawing water from wells and eating mangoes by plucking them from trees.

In the entire village, he was known as 'Mota (Fatso)'. Bright shining eyes, a mop of thick hair, round hanging cheeks and stomach—Hari was not a child who could be missed easily, or missed at all! Overwhelmed by love, his grandmother believed it was her personal responsibility to ensure that Hari ate properly as his mother was not around. She fed him everything she could find—large glasses of milk (that came from the family cows), food made in desi ghee, fruits and whatnot. To give Hari his due, he attacked every kind of food and drink with such zeal that it helped him retain his nickname for several years!

There was a general belief amongst the village folk that if they wanted to bring a warm, happy smile to the face of Hanumandas Kanoria, they needed to reach out to Hari. If the saying—the way to a man's heart is through his stomach—could be altered to 'the way to a grandfather's heart is through his grandson', it would fit Hanumandas perfectly. Rasgullas, gulab jamuns and sweetmeats of all sizes and shapes would show up almost magically every morning at the Kanoria home and our dear Mota Hari gorged on them with enthusiasm. He believed in equality right from a tender age, that is, each variety of sweetmeat had to be shown equal love and respect. So he ate them all, without any discrimination whatsoever, none at all!

Behind their home was a verdant garden with a variety of fruit trees like mangoes, guavas and berries. Despite his weight, Hari was extremely agile and it took him very little effort to scamper up the tallest of trees. Seated on a branch he would pluck fruits and throw them down for his little friends who would run around collecting all the goodies from heaven, which Hari unearthed for them. Our beloved Hari remained at the top while relishing the nectar of life.

Young Hari had a belly laugh, a happy demeanour and a sharing nature. This endeared him to the young boys of the village and he was rather popular. Benevolence was not an attitude, but a way of being for him, and Hari would share everything he had with his friends. Often a group of 5 or 6 of them would cover distances of as much as six km on a single bicycle! Sometimes walking and talking, sometimes running and panting, sometimes one on top of the other on the little cycle, pedalling through their carefree childhood for all it was worth.

Standing (from left to right): Shribhagwan and Hari. Sitting (from left to right): Kamla, Saroj, Hari's mother Bhagirathi Devi, with Hemant as a toddler, and Kanta. (Hari's younger sister Bimla is missing as being the eldest among sisters, she was married by the time this photograph was taken)

Chapter 3
Seeds of Spirituality

As per the Vedic tradition, the right age to start learning about spirituality and its impact on our life is from birth itself. And this is what happened to Hari. Spirituality is not about rituals and traditions, but about right living. And Hari had the opportunity to observe his grandparents at close quarters. Hari would accompany his grandfather to the temple each morning and grew up worshipping Lord Shiva and Goddess Durga. Even as a child he would offer flowers to the deities, tossing them energetically, and ring the bell with great enthusiasm.

The vibrations of the temple at the Kanoria home attracted people from far and wide. On every special occasion, the deities would be brought all the way from Calcutta. Dressed and bejewelled, they would be placed in the temple. Hanumandas would hold the chubby little hands of Hari and teach him to conduct all the rituals in the right manner. People of all ages—children, teenagers, adults and the elderly—would come for the festivals and celebrate together with great enthusiasm.

Watching the way his grandfather conducted himself and the pujas, made young Hari aware of the grace of God. God ceased to be just a statue made of rock and clay—rather, He became an ignited presence in the mind and heart of the young Hari.

Whenever Hari thought of his grandparents, the words of one of his favourite Bengali poets, Guru Rabindranath Tagore, came alive in his mind:

> This is my prayer to thee, my Lord: strike, strike at the root of penury in my heart.

Give me the strength lightly to bear my joys and sorrows.
Give me the strength to make my love fruitful in service.
Give me the strength never to disown the poor or bend my knees before insolent might.
Give me the strength to raise my mind high above daily trifles.
And give me the strength to surrender my strength to thy will with love.

Hari's mother Bhagirathi was a person steeped in spirituality

Learning at the feet of his father, Kedarnath

The temple in Barhiya

Chapter 4

Much Like a Tree

As Hari closely observed his grandfather and the way he conducted himself, one of the aspects about Hanumandas that struck a deep chord within him was his humility. The Kanoria family had created enormous wealth and his grandfather was an affluent man by any means, but he lived a simple life.

He had every imaginable comfort at his disposal—vehicles ranging from an Austin car to a Victorian carriage (both open as well as closed), acres of agricultural land and even a power plant in the house—yet never was this wealth kept for the family alone. Whenever, wherever possible, it was used for the welfare of others. Hanumandas never snubbed anyone. The electricity generated by their power plant helped light the village temple.

Hanumandas spoke with love and respect to everyone, rich or poor, child or adult. Hari Prasad remembers one incident clearly. Hanumandas, who was walking back home after a day's hard work, came across a fruit seller. Very affectionately Hanumandas asked him, 'So how many did you sell today?' The fruit seller replied humbly, 'Babu, today was a tough day. I have not sold anything.' Immediately Hanumandas told him, 'Leave the entire basket with me, the family will consume the fruits. Take this money and go give your wife some good news instead of saying you sold nothing.' Little Hari watched their exchange in rapt attention, observing and absorbing everything.

Hari loved watching Hanumandas at work. Every day after the puja, the duo would go to the lentil manufacturing unit belonging to the family. Hanumandas would enquire about the production and supervise the construction projects, preparing his ward for the trials and tribulations that would come his way.

One important attribute of Hanumandas, which Hari imbibed very early on, was complete surrender to God and His ways. Hanumandas etched this into little Hari's heart, mind and soul: The success they saw was God's grace; they were mere instruments, and to become arrogant about it would be a folly indeed. In the same way, the trials and tribulations that came their way were also sent by God and He would find a solution too. The role of each individual was to work hard and remain humble. The rest was all a play of the Almighty's hand—sometimes in favour, sometimes not so much. Everything was to be accepted and dealt with in a graceful manner.

The garden in the backyard of their home was a temple of learning for the little boy. Hari spent many happy hours here, digging his hands into the soil, tending to plants, learning gardening. One day as he sat there, it struck him that his grandfather was much like the trees he so loved. Deeply rooted to the soil and yet aspiring to the sky.

Hari's grandfather Hanumandas Kanoria

Chapter 5

Why Waste?

Diwali was celebrated in the Kanoria household with great pomp and splendour. Hundreds of diyas would be lit around the haveli, sweetmeats of several kinds would be made, people would be fed, crackers would be burst and there would be prolonged pujas to the Goddess, with everyone singing and chanting in unison with devotion. In fact, Diwali would visit the family almost a month before Diwali, so elaborate were the preparations.

In Kolkata, one year large cans of oils were brought to light the numerous diyas and stored for usage in Diwali. Hari was roaming around the house wondering what to do next when his eyes fell on the cans. He sniffed, he touched, he licked—and realized it was oil.

Why not try making a swimming pool out of oil for a change?

Lo and behold, he dragged the cans to the balcony, shut the door and tipped them. The oil spilled, spreading all over the floor, much to little Hari's excitement. He clapped and laughed, and with a chuckle he jumped into the pool of oil with such style that would have put the best swimmers to shame.

The next few moments could only be described as a slice of heaven for young Hariya. He lay on his round belly; he flailed his arms and legs, turning around and acting as though he was floating on oil. The oil spread in the balcony were his own Olympic-sized pool and he made the most of it.

His fantasy world came to an abrupt end when he heard a loud scream. It was his mother. She was watching him with blazing eyes. 'What is wrong with you, Hariya? What have you done!' Hari got the dressing-down of his life—as his mother yelled at him for wasting all that oil. She wept and asked him, 'Tell me Hariya, how do we celebrate Diwali without oil?' She had to order more tins of oil.

Hari heard his mother out sheepishly. His young mind had comprehended the message clearly. What he had done was wrong because of the wastage. The oil was to be used for lighting the diyas and by spilling it over the floor he had rendered it useless. He understood the value of not wasting anything loud and clear. His mother had ensured that the lesson learnt remained for a lifetime.

Even now, so many decades later, one can see that while the Kanoria home speaks of abundance, wastage is a strict no-no. In fact, Hari distinctly remembers how both his grandmother and mother used to pour water on their thalis after finishing their meals and drink the same water. These experiences left their impact on him—later becoming a multi crore business in itself, of generating wealth from waste.

Ah, the memories of childhood! Some last a lifetime. And the lessons? They last for eternity.

The excitement in Hari Prasad as he spoke about this incident was palpable. It was clear that though his mother's firing had had its effect on him, he didn't regret his oil pool saga even for an instant. But then if he had had a dull childhood, you wouldn't be reading his story, would you?

Chapter 6

Walking the Thin Line

Hari was a restless child. He had no fear of anyone or anything. An explorer at heart, he would often find himself in strange situations. He could almost smell mischief from afar, and like a dog that had sniffed a bone he would scamper to sites where some adventure could be found—and unearthed them.

One day he was at a construction site, a perfect setting for a curious child waiting for something to happen. With his eyes gleaming with joy, he explored the entire area. Who would have known that in the years to come, infrastructure would become a calling for him? That the time spent playing with mud, brick and cement, and interacting with labourers would develop his acumen for realty to a point where standing in a room he could give its exact measurements and indicate the material used to build it without any help from a professional or an instrument.

To come back to young Hari, the brat took a stick and tapped on the wall, smelt the cement, threw a brick here and there. And then he saw something that finally made his heart leap with joy. There was an unfinished wall, about fifteen feet high. Without thinking and without analysing, off he went, climbing, slipping, a foot here, a hand there, until he was on the top.

Once he reached there, he found that the wall was narrower than he had anticipated. Even that did not daunt the spirit of our Hariya. Instead of being scared, he started walking across the 15-inch wide wall at a height of fifteen feet—imagining himself to be a trapeze artist.

From far away Hari's grandfather saw the scene. His heart

was in his mouth—was that really his grandson walking on such a narrow and high wall? One slip and it could lead to several broken bones.

Hanumandas went running towards the wall and gently told Hari, 'Come down, I want to speak to you.' The calm but strict tone tamed Hari and the next moment, with the dexterity of a baby monkey, he was at ground level, looking into his grandfather's eyes. He expected a thrashing, and on seeing the height of the wall from below he realized the risk he had just taken.

Hanumandas did not scream or hit Hari. Rather, with a lot of love and tenderness he explained the risk in what Hari had just attempted. He spelled out what could have happened with just a little slip. Expressing his love for his grandson, he requested him to always keep his life, and his safety, paramount.

Hari nodded vigorously.

As he watched his grandfather's retreating figure, a silhouette against the sunset, Hari was filled with love and wonder. Even at the young age he could fathom the maturity of his grandfather. Had his grandfather alarmed him or screamed at him, he might have lost his footing and got hurt. He had so wisely and gently asked him to come down and only then explained the situation.

For Hari, it was a lesson well learnt: In any alarming situation, keep your cool. Focus first on getting the person concerned out of harm's way and only then do what needs to be done. Creating panic will not help. Decades later, whenever business went awry, Hari kept this message close to his heart and took each step with maturity and thoughtfulness.

I loved the way Hari Prasad's eyes shone as he shared this experience. I also realized that life teaches us lessons in so many ways, at so many stages. A good student is one who learns what needs to be learnt, without fuss and remembers it for a lifetime.

Chapter 7

Bullying the Bully

There was a notorious bully in their Calcutta neighbourhood where the Kanorias lived. All the children feared him for he not only looked bigger and stronger, but also didn't hesitate to give a whack here or pull an ear there as per his whims and fancies. He was notorious for all the damage he could cause to others with his words and his hands.

The children shivered when he came to the park or some common area—they knew he was the tyrant and they mere subjects; everything would pan out as per his commands and desires.

When Hari visited Calcutta, his cousins and siblings told him about 'The Bully'. He did not like the fear he saw on their faces and decided to take matters into his capable albeit chubby hands.

The two met on the terrace of their building and looked at each other with bloodthirsty eyes. Hari turned out to be the stronger of the two. The bully of Calcutta had finally met his match in our Hariya from Barhiya. His ego was shattered as he was beaten black and blue.

After the fight was over, Hari realized that if the elders found out about this, they would beat him for being so naughty. So he put on his thinking cap and ran as fast as his chubby legs could carry him to his residence on Vivekananda Road, and hid inside the water tank on the terrace. It had a couple of feet of water.

Hari remained in the water tank for almost two to three hours blocking off the water supply to the residents. When a few of them came up to check the tank, they discovered Hari in it!

His family members were informed and they immediately rushed to the terrace and pleaded with him to come out.

From inside the tank Hari negotiated, 'Promise me, you will not beat me. Only then will I come out!' The family members hesitatingly gave their word. Only when he had all the reassurance he needed—that not a hair on his head would be touched—did the victorious, dripping warrior come out with a big grin.

He had bullied the bully.

He continues to do that to this day, whether the bullies come in the form of lawyers, politicians, policemen or those who try to play the mischief in business.

The bully must be bullied at any cost. Hari had learnt that long back.

Chapter 8

Go Green

The large garden behind Hari's house in Barhiya had a huge mango tree which was almost twenty feet high. Many an afternoon would see Hari scampering around the garden, digging with a stick, adding fertilizers in plants and, yes, climbing his big, beloved mango tree and getting a view of beautiful Barhiya right from the top—with all its colourful residents appearing like miniature dolls from where he sat.

Everything about the garden seemed to entice Hari—from the sunshine falling on the green leaves to the fragrance of the soil; from the blossoming of a flower to the gradual decaying and subsequent dying of a plant. The way one studies in school, Hari loved to study in the garden. He observed the life cycles of the plants and tried to learn what could be done to help the plants grow better—and live longer.

There were a few gardeners who had been hired to keep this patch of paradise bountiful. Hari would watch them closely to see if they were doing the work well. Even as a young boy he was quite a task master.

Once he observed that one of the gardeners was not watering the plants properly. He immediately caught hold of him and asked him why he was not doing a good job. The lazy gardener immediately blamed the well and said it was very difficult to draw out water from it so he could not do his job as expected.

Hari, who looked upon the plants like his own little brothers and sisters, couldn't accept such tardiness. He immediately took the bucket and told the gardener to watch him. Within minutes, one after the other, Hari drew close to hundred buckets of water.

He then summoned the gardener and said, 'If at this young age I can draw so much water and that too in such a short time, surely you can do the same.'

Then he sat below his dear mango tree and watched as the gardener huffed and puffed, cribbed and complained but finally drew water out just the way Hari wanted.

Hanumandas's ways were soft and gentle; Hari was loud and boisterous in his mannerism. The staff at the Kanoria house learnt to deal with both temperaments because they knew the underlying factor, for both, was always love.

Chapter 9

The Power of Prayer

One day Hari was drawing water from the well in their old ancestral home. Just then a young girl of about 10 or 12 came and stood near the well. The water of the well was very sweet and people from far and wide came to the Kanoria home to draw water from it as it was believed to be pure.

For Hari, being at the well and having a bath was so enjoyable that he actually lost himself completely in the moment. He was engrossed in his thoughts and did not even realize that when he threw the rope into the well to draw water, somehow the girl got entangled in it and fell inside.

She began to scream and cry and that's when Hari realized what had happened. Fortunately, she held on to the chain that lowered the bucket into the well and managed to hang on for dear life.

Meanwhile, Hari ran and called people for help. All the while he kept praying to Ma Jagdamba that nothing should happen to the girl as he hadn't been aware of what he was doing. That his ignorance should not hurt anyone was the prayer on his lips. With the grace of Ma Jagdamba, within moments the girl was rescued.

It was a day that Hari would never forget because unknowingly he had discovered something beautiful—faith in action and prayer. He realized that when a situation went beyond his control, he had to do two things simultaneously. One was to take action and do his best to get out of the unfavourable situation, the way he had raced to ask for help as soon as he grasped that he couldn't get the girl out all by himself. The second thing was to pray to the

Lord to protect him, the way he had prayed to Ma Jagdamba in his moment of sheer panic.

This combination of action and faith helped him when he was merely a child. It continues to help him even at eighty.

Chapter 10

Ma to Ma Kali

As Hari entered his teens, he began to deeply appreciate the ways of his grandmother. He watched her and his admiration for her grew on several accounts.

Firstly, despite there being a coterie of servants who were paid well, she continued to live in a humble way. She also insisted on serving food to the 20-plus members of the household with her own hands. She believed it was her dharma and that the food served by her hands contained love and warmth which would do wonders for the family members partaking it.

Secondly, Hari saw how beautifully his grandmother got along with all the other women of the village and her family. Irrespective of their class or creed, their financial status or physical appearance, she would treat everyone the same. Every morning a big group of women would go to the Ganga for the morning ablutions. There would be laughter in the air as all of them would share nuggets about their lives, the day's gossip and whatnot.

He also thoroughly enjoyed watching the way she conducted the Chhath puja, a festival celebrated in a significant way in Bihar. It is a time to worship the Sun God and his sister, Chhathi Maiya, for bestowing their bounties on the earth. It is also believed that if the seeker has certain desires and prays ardently during this period, their wishes are granted.

Chhath puja was considered to be significant in the Kanoria home as well. Hari would watch his grandmother get ready for the sacred days in several ways—through fasting, abstinence and worship. One of the rituals of the puja was to go to the Ganga but not on foot. From their home to the Ganga, he would watch his grandmother prostrate herself on the ground and roll all the way. He saw his mother do the same in Calcutta.

He was amused once when he saw his mother, who was known mainly for her love, tenderness and gentleness, become a spitfire and take to task a policeman who was being a hindrance to the performance of the Chhath puja. That the woman who readily invested hours and hours in serving her family was equally capable of assuming the role of Ma Kali, when required, impressed Hari.

He realized that a woman had many faces—she could be the gentle hand that rocks the cradle and, equally, the heat of the blazing sun which could destroy wrongdoing. Hari learnt to respect the various sides of a woman watching his grandmother first and his mother next.

Hari's paternal grandmother, Banarasi Devi

Chapter 11

The End of an Era

Hari's grandfather had two sons living in Barhiya who grew alongside the young boy. They were five years and one-and-a-half years older than Hari respectively. Hanumandas was much closer to Hari, his eldest grandson, than his sons. There is a saying that the interest earned is even dearer than the original investment. No wonder Hari was the apple of his grandfather's eye. The beauty and simplicity of Hanumandas could never be overestimated.

He made do with only three pairs of dhoti and kurta till the end of his life. Whenever his eldest daughter-in-law got him an extra set, for an occasion like a wedding or festival, he would immediately ask, 'What is the need for this? I already have enough.'

To be so wealthy and yet so simple and humble but not a miser—touched Hari deeply.

Although there were many caregivers, Hanumandas liked to have Hari massage his feet every night. He firmly believed in humility and the value of relationships, and he felt that youngsters would learn to respect the elderly only if they served them. He knew an important principle of life: One gets attached to that which one serves. And in serving each other, he believed, the family members would feel closer to one another. Neither did he hesitate to extend himself to anyone, nor did he mind asking someone to do the same for him.

One night Hari after having pressed his grandfather's feet lovingly was about to leave the room when suddenly Hanumandas got up, and cried out, 'Hari, Hari!' Within moments he collapsed and left his human form.

As 16-year-old Hari saw the lifeless body of his idol, mentor and in so many ways his best friend, he burst out crying. Hanumandas was quite young (about fifty-five or so) and to lose someone that important so unexpectedly was quite a blow for Hari.

In many ways, Hari Prasad Kanoria believes, the death of his grandfather changed his life overnight. From being a young, carefree lad roaming through Barhiya with gay abandon, he suddenly became a mature young man who keenly felt his responsibility towards everyone and everything that his grandfather had left behind.

He suddenly felt the need to grow up—for his family and himself. Death changes lives in mystical ways. And for Hari, too, it was no different.

Chapter 12

Swami and Me

After his paternal grandfather's demise, young Hari stayed in the village to finish his schooling and then shifted back to Calcutta to be under the tutelage of his parents. He had four brothers and three sisters, and the siblings fought, squabbled, argued as much as they loved each other.

Once Hari's father had to go to Banares on some important work and he took ill over there. One by one each of the children went and stayed with Kedarnath to take care of him.

Hari fondly remembers going by a small nauka (boat) across the Ganga to a place where his father went would get a massage. He would chit-chat with the young boatman and the two forged a strange but intimate bond. So much so that once when there was a sudden flash flood and it looked like the boat might capsize, the young boatman told the strong Hari, 'Don't worry, Babu, I will save you.' Hari had a good laugh because the boy was slight in build and didn't even know how to swim! But such were the little tales of love in Hari's life—and they made everything so meaningful.

Hari also remembers that it was in Banares that his lifelong love for books began. His father would give him a few rupees and say, use it well. He would add, 'The best way to use this money is to buy books!'

Hari would go running to the market and find books of all kinds to read. *Chandamama* and *Reader's Digest* were his favourite. In an era when education itself was a question mark, the children of the Kanoria home were reading books that gave them not just knowledge but also a worldview.

It was here that he discovered books on Swami Vivekananda—which shaped his entire life in the most beautiful ways. The quotes, the stories and the poetry of Swamiji have always come to Hari's aid through all his trials and tribulations, always giving him the wisdom he needed when he needed it.

Hari remembers the poem, 'Quest for God', by Swami Vivekananda that is etched into every cell of his being:

O'ver hill and dale and mountain range,
In temple, church, and mosque,
In Vedas, Bible, Al Koran
I had searched for Thee in vain.

Like a child in the wildest forest lost
I have cried and cried alone,
'Where art Thou gone, my God, my love?
The echo answered, 'gone'.

And days and nights and years then passed
A fire was in the brain,
I knew not when day changed in night
The heart seemed rent in twain.

I laid me down on Ganges's shore,
Exposed to sun and rain;
With burning tears I laid the dust
And wailed with waters' roar.

I called on all the holy names
Of every clime and creed.
'Show me the way, in mercy, ye
Great ones who have reached the goal.'

Years then passed in bitter cry,
Each moment seemed an age,
Till one day midst my cries and groans
Some one seemed calling me.

A gentle soft and soothing voice
That said 'my son' 'my son',
That seemed to thrill in unison
With all the chords of my soul.

I stood on my feet and tried to find
The place the voice came from;
I searched and searched and turned to see
Round me, before, behind,
Again, again it seemed to speak
The voice divine to me.
In rapture all my soul was hushed,
Entranced, enthralled in bliss.

A flash illumined all my soul;
The heart of my heart opened wide.
O joy, O bliss, what do I find!
My love, my love you are here
And you are here, my love, my all!

And I was searching thee-
From all eternity you were there
Enthroned in majesty!
From that day forth, wherever I roam,
I feel Him standing by
O'ver hill and dale, high mount and vale,
Far far away and high.

The moon's soft light, the stars so bright,
The glorious orb of day,
He shines in them; His beauty—might—
Reflected lights are they.
The majestic morn, the melting eve,
The boundless billowing sea,
In nature's beauty, songs of birds,
I see through them—it is He.

When dire calamity seizes me,
The heart seems weak and faint,
All nature seems to crush me down,
With laws that never bend.
Meseems I hear Thee whispering sweet
My love, 'I am near', 'I am near'.
My heart gets strong. With thee, my love,
A thousand deaths no fear.
Thou speakest in the mother's lay
Thou shuts the babies eye,
When innocent children laugh and play,
I see Thee standing by.

When holy friendship shakes the hand,
He stands between them too;
He pours the nectar in mother's kiss
And the baby's sweet 'mama'.
Thou wert my God with prophets old,
All creeds do come from Thee,
The Vedas, Bible, and Koran bold
Sing Thee in Harmony.

'Thou art, 'Thou art' the Soul of souls
In the rushing stream of life.
'Om tat sat om.' Thou art my God,
My love, I am thine, I am thine.

Chapter 13

All For One and One For All

When Hari returned to Calcutta it was time for him to join college. He was accompanied by his cousin Shyam Sunder, uncle Ramavatar, and a friend from the village, Atmaram. The family provided them with a study room next to the family office which was located in 132, Cotton Street.

That is how things were for the Kanorias.

No one was made to feel like an outsider. There was no special service given to someone just because he or she was family—everyone was equal. If Hari has to be honest with himself, while growing up, the very word family seemed to have blurred lines. Wasn't the distant uncle as special as his own brother? Wasn't the friend from the village who stayed with them, like a cousin?

Though these looked like normal happenings, they helped shape in the Kanorias an important attitude and culture: of unity among diversity, of love and brotherhood among all, and of oneness, no matter who the other is.

If there is one thing that always strikes me about Hari Prasad, it is his ability to make you feel you are his, no matter who you are. I have seen him play with children, and I have watched him at work; I have seen him among people of different religions and political stature—with each person, he is one in spirit. I believe this is not just a part of an attitude or culture for him. It runs deeper than blood, too. It's probably in his DNA itself.

Hari with his uncles, aunts, brother and his wife

Chapter 14
Fat to Fit

Besides giving Hari the right upbringing, Barhiya also played an integral role in giving him layers and layers of extra fat. Since he knew he would be joining some college in Calcutta, Hari became very conscious of his obesity. It began to haunt him as he felt that all the college students would make fun of him.

He had hit a happy century in terms of weight when he decided enough was enough. His heart was set on becoming fitter. Since Hari's biggest weakness was food, especially sweets, it was not an easy feat. And yet Hari trained his mind—no matter what, he would lose weight.

Cycling, running, playing, exercising and complete control over food led him to lose close to thirty kilos in two years' time. He was a healthy and acceptable seventy kilos when he finally joined college.

This entire exercise taught Hari the value of health. He realized that the very first God that everyone needed to pray to, and respect, was their body. Without that nothing else was possible. The value of a physical fitness regimen and the importance of the right kind of food eaten at the right intervals was something that Hari taught himself during this phase, without any dietician's plan. He was neither starving nor fasting. His grandmother looked at this phase with love, and some amount of amusement, at how her darling 'mota' grandson had begun to train himself by saying no to potatoes, rice and sweets. Of course, once in a while when 'prasad' was offered to him with a lot of love, he wouldn't deny it.

It is a delight to see Hari Prasad take care of his health even now when he is in his eighties. Early in the morning he can be seen doing yoga in his room and thereafter taking a walk in the garden. Be it the Agri-Horticultural Garden or the Victoria Memorial, you can watch him huffing and puffing, walking at a crazy speed and still saying a booming hello to passersby, and checking on the well-being of all the known people.

At home I have seen him eat plates and plates of fruits. His all-time favourite dessert is mishti doi—which he makes with gud instead of sugar. So proud is he of his recipe that when people come from far and wide, he shares it with them as though parting with his best-kept secret and is also known to pack a spoonful of it for guests so they can use it in their homes. Laughter is an integral part of his health regimen and I hear his booming laughter several times in a day.

There is also a large massage chair placed in his room—and he enjoys the different massages it offers. He looks no less than a king on his throne as he sits there, loudly giving instructions to his many staff boys on how things should be done properly. Some things never change, I guess.

Chapter 15

Carpe Diem!

When in Calcutta, Hari did not find it too difficult to adapt to his life in the city. One of his greatest strengths was adaptability. When in Barhiya, one would think he was a country boy, born and bred in the village—Barhiya boy; and, when in Calcutta, he quickly took on the hues of the city and its life and became one among the city folk.

He would fight a lot with his siblings—but the underlying current would always be love. And yet it was a lot for the mother to handle. She would scold him when he troubled the siblings. He especially had a lot of verbal duels with his sister Bimla who would ask him, 'Bhaiya, if I die will you be able to buy a new me even for as little as 1 paisa in the market? Do not fight with me!'

He happened to read somewhere that 'bhujiya' (a crispy snack) was not got for health and would fight with all his siblings to ensure they don't eat it. He was even willing to make them cry—it was for their good—and Hari's mother was always at her wits' end trying to manage him. She would often tell him, 'Hariya, let them eat, what will happen? Let them enjoy. Do not trouble them so much.'

Hari made great friends in Calcutta. He distinctly remembers a wonderful walk home from school—the friends were laughing, joking and gossiping—when suddenly there was a downpour. Since they were in an area which got waterlogged very quickly, they were a little stunned to see the water level rise at an alarming rate.

Hari and his friends quickly tucked their books under their shirts and instead of being afraid of the rising water level they danced, swam, sang their way back home, drenched in the bliss of boyhood.

One of the common underlying thread I sensed in almost every story that Hari Prasad regaled me with was an ability to go with the flow. He did not think too much, he did not analyse too much; he was not afflicted by shadows of the past or with a fear of the future—wherever he was, in that moment he made the most of what it was. In that sense, Hari Prasad was always with the flow. I admire this trait very much and have learnt that instead of thinking so much about life, I should perhaps simply start living it.

Chapter 16

The Right Word

The dictionary meaning of the word 'habit' is 'a settled or regular tendency or practice, especially one that is hard to give up.' Hari believed that a lot of what he got right in his later years was the boon of certain habits cultivated in his early years.

Hari's father believed that his children should have a good command of the English language. Being a visionary, he was sure English was the future of the world and wanted all his children to be well-versed in it. He himself had won the award for being the best student of his batch at the Presidency College. In fact, the first President of India, Dr Rajendra Prasad, was the best student of his batch at Presidency College as well.

Hari's father completed his under graduation from Presidency College, with a First Division. After the unfortunate demise of his father, Kedarnath, being the eldest son, became the head of the family. Aided by his intellect, wisdom and a flair for entrepreneurship, Kedarnath took on all the responsibilities at a young age. Even while Hari was in school in Barhiya, his father and his Gita teacher had seen to it that Hari would read, write and speak English. In a little village where education was as rare and precious as water in a desert, here was a young boy who pretty much exemplified what the superstar Amitabh Bachchan said in one of his movies, 'I can talk English, I can walk English, I can laugh English because English is a very funny language.'

Jokes apart, Kedarnath wanted Hari to pen his thoughts. He bought him a beautiful hard-bound leather diary and asked him to write in it every day. At first Hari wondered what he would find to write each day. Was there so much happening in a day, and in his life, to document it each day?

However, as time passed by, his writing transformed—from a habit to a hobby, from a hobby to a passion, and from a passion to a profession. Not a day went by when Hari wouldn't write. It had helped him to get admission in a premier college of India, Presidency College. Dr Bimal Jalan, former governor of the Reserve Bank of India, as well as Dr Ramgopal Agarwala, a member of Niti Aayog, studied with him. In his free time, he would go swimming in a nearby club. He would also spend time with his friends at the Coffee House, an adda for students and professors.

However, no matter how busy he was, writing became an integral part of his life. The world around him aided him. For example, one of his teachers at Presidency, Prof. Sengupta, took an intense liking for Hari and advised him to read and write hundred pages each day which Hari would, with great zeal.

He realized, the more he wrote, the more exciting he found his life to be. Life, like writing, ceased to be moments passing by intangibly; it became, instead, a string of words and sentences leading somewhere.

Hari would attempt stories, poems and even songs, and a large and happy part of his growing-up years consisted of penning his experiences, bringing them from the realm of thoughts to the hard-bound diaries.

He also read different genres. His favourite English writer was Erle Stanley Gardner, the creator of the popular character Perry Mason, a criminal defence lawyer. For days and nights Hari would sometimes remain engrossed in books, and for hours nothing would exist but him and words, words and him—all lost in a magical wonderland.

One of his favourite books was *The Robe* by Lloyd C. Douglas which basically gave the message that no matter where the problems came from, there was always a solution to be found. He still remembers the sentences which meant: Calamities never come alone. When calamities seize me, God opens a door as a saviour.

Chapter 17

The Rebel

It was in 1957 that Hari joined the prestigious Presidency College in Calcutta. As he walked through the sprawling campus, he felt a great sense of pride at how far a boy born in the small village of Barhiya had come. He rubbed shoulders with some of the finest students there and realized just how handy it was to have a good command of English. He fit right in because of his good communication and writing skills, thanks to the foresight his father and teacher had shown.

A part of Hari loved to always fit in. However, a part of him also loved to stand out. Among all the young men smartly dressed in pants and shirts, shoes shining till they reflected one's face, Hari had the courage to do something totally different. He wore khadi kurta and dhoti to college along with two Bengali students to protest against westernization, representing his staunch love for Bharat Mata. He was deeply inspired by Rishi Aurobindo's words: 'I have three madnesses… love for mother, love for nation and love for God.'

He was a patriot at heart and even as people succumbed to peer pressure in terms of dressing or mannerism, Hari remained extremely proud of his Bihari accent as well as his Indian clothing. If someone asked him about it, he would say, 'I am an Indian and I will dress Indian.'

In a college filled with students blindly aping western culture, here was a youngster along with a few friends who was nothing short of a swadesi movement in himself.

Hari just didn't like to do as expected. He would go beyond

or completely the other way. One couldn't box Hari. Oh no, some people are not meant to be defined predictably—or confined.

As I heard about this incident, I realized something. It seems so small, right? Dressing differently—that's about it, on the face of it. But when you really think about it—it takes a tremendous amount of courage and conviction to do something which is not the norm, and everyone else is questioning it. To still retain your originality is a great feat.

I also realized that the seeds of a great businessman are sown during his young days. The ability to think like no one else and stand your ground are such essential aspects of becoming an entrepreneur—not once, not twice, but multiple times you will be asked to show that you mean what you say and say what you mean, even if no one else in the whole wide world believes it. Your business is your innermost dream, the expression of your quietest whisper, and no one except you can hear it at times.

Graduation in Law

Chapter 18

Get It Done!

After a couple of years of being in Presidency College, Hari's father urged him to get a transfer to St Xavier's College. The idea was to go to a morning college so that Hari could work during the day, learning the ropes of business. Xavier's was as well-known and acclaimed as Presidency in those days.

However, to instantly get admission in Xavier's, was no mean feat. Students from across India waited for months to get in. In the middle of the year, with no connection or reference, how would Hari get in?

Hari had a unique plan.

Every single morning he would go to the college and sit outside the principal's office. At that time a respectable, fine gentleman called Father Joris was presiding over the college. As Principal Joris would come out of his office he would see the young and charismatic Hari stand up, bow and greet him with a huge smile, saying, 'Good afternoon Father Joris!' Father would smile, greet and carry on.

This went on for days. Finally, Father Joris got curious—as Hari wanted, and asked him, 'Son, every morning you come and greet me. Can I do something for you?'

Hari's heart was beating against his chest. Finally, the many morning prayers (and greetings) stood a chance of being answered. Very humbly Hari explained that he wanted to join as a student of Xavier's so he could work alongside. Father Joris liked the young boy's attitude, persistence and ability to think out of the box. Such were the students who would do Xavier's proud.

He immediately asked Hari to come to his room and got the

administration to take the necessary steps towards his admission.

Soon after, Hari walked into Xavier's College.

It was a new beginning for young Hari—working along with learning.

Tenacity is an important trait of any legend. In situations where most ordinary people give up, those who rise to the extraordinary, refuse to give up. This little instance is endearing and heart-warming but it also reflects Hari's spirit of never-say-die attitude and his ability to keep trying till he got what he wanted. While I smiled as he shared the story, I became a little more resolute towards my dreams.

Graduation from St Xavier's

Chapter 19

Sweet Money

Like most young men, Hari too wished to get his driving licence. He went along with a few friends to take the trial test. There was a system in those days of giving some money called 'sweet money' to the people in the licensing authority so they could buy sweets for their family—and, in turn, you would get your driving licence.

Hari refused to bribe. He felt why should he have to do all that when he was good at driving and deserved his licence?

He was in for a shock when his friends received their licences, but he did not. He asked his friends what they had done differently, and they replied with barely suppressed smiles, 'We took the trial test just like you. But we also gave the sweet money.'

In this way, for two continuous years Hari was denied his licence simply because he refused to give the 'sweet money'!

His father watched Hari get frustrated, and asked, 'What happened, Son, why are you not getting your licence? Have you not learnt driving?' Hari replied, 'I have learnt driving, Father, and I am a very good driver! It is because I have not given the "sweet money"?'

Kedarnath had a good laugh and then said to his adamant son, 'Hari, it is just a small show of respect for the person's family. Don't be foolish, and please give it.'

That year Hari handed over the 'sweet money' and, within a few days, he received his licence!

This may look like a simple incident, but it was not. Hari realized something of great importance. He realized that sometimes logic didn't work. There was no reason to over-analyse everything.

Chapter 20

A Book in Time

Buddham saranam gacchami
Dhammam saranam gacchami
Sangham saranam gacchami

The above saying means,

> I go to the Buddha (The higher consciousness) for refuge
> I go to the dhamma (His teachings) for refuge
> I go to the sangha (community) for refuge

In many ways, Hari had already found a refuge in higher consciousness. The teachings of life too were being followed, consciously or unconsciously, owing to a great upbringing. It was now time to follow the third principle—of having a sangha, or community, in place.

I am sure most of us have experienced the role that close friends play in our life—especially if they are both like-minded as well as right-minded. They act as a balm for the pain, calm us through the storms and are a sounding board for all our goals and dreams. It was in Xavier's that Hari made several close friends, who would stand the test of time for decades to come.

Some notable ones among them are Mohan Lal Bajaj, Babu Lal Agarwala, Shanti Sukhani and Amarendranath Jain. Krishna Kumar Nevatia from

Krishna Kumar Nevatia

Scottish College ran a homeopathic shop near Bagree market and since Hari had a fascination for homeopathy from a very young age, the two became great friends. In fact, it was with him that Hari developed a love for spiritual Bengali films and plays being held at Star Theatre.

Hari also loved to distribute books on spiritual leaders like Swami Vivekananda and Sri Ramakrishna Paramhamsa to others. He believed that no matter how young one was, one could still play a part in the spiritual evolution of the world by sharing good books, good words and good thoughts with others.

This habit has remained intact to this day. If you happen to meet Hari Prasad Kanoria at his office or home, he will not let you leave without a few good books that could potentially change your life forever.

Although I do have a few friends from my school and college days with whom I am still in touch, I am not sure if decades down the line we will continue to relate. It was wonderful for me to see the ways in which Hari Prasad Kanoria nurtures his relationships, making him so loved and popular among his friends—friends who have more than stood the test of time.

Hari's friends—lifelong relationships. From left to right: Mohan Bajaj, Prem Chand Jaiswal, Babulal Agarwala, Shantilal Chopra, Hari Prasad Kanoria, Shanti Sukhani, Om Prakash Saraogi and Jugal Kishore Sarda

Chapter 21

The Joy of Small Things

Hari shared a unique relationship with each of his friends. One such friend was Om Prakash Saraogi. One day Om was waiting at the bus stop and Hari was driving past—on his way to work. As soon as Hari saw Om, he immediately stopped the car and offered him a lift. Om said he would manage on his own, but Hari didn't listen. He dropped Om to his destination even though it was in a completely opposite direction from his own. A small incident, but it stayed with Om for decades. Friendship is like that, isn't it? It's often not the one big thing, but the numerous little things that just stay with people.

Another incident Om remembers is when Hari had invited all his friends home for dinner. Being slightly shy Om told him, Hari that he had already eaten. Hari could clearly see through his awkwardness and immediately told the maharaj (cook) to get snacks for Om and ensured he ate before Hari.

Yet another friend, Shantilal Chopra, shares how Hari takes relationships seriously. It was Shanti's younger sister's wedding. Hari's immediate relative was also getting married on the same day. And yet he took time out from his own chores and responsibilities and made it a point to attend the wedding. His gesture touched Shanti. He says, 'He could have missed it. Who would have held it against him? He had a genuine reason. But that is not the way Hari functions. He thinks from his heart and is always there for his close friends.'

S.C. Sukhani, Hari's friend from Xavier's College recalls how each Sunday the friends would meet at Hari's home to chat and have discussions on various matters, including studies! He remembers how Hari would always be a great host and ensure all his friends were fed to their heart's content. So many decades later, he still remembers the delicious, piping hot pakodas and Ganguram's sandesh served at the Kanoria home. He also recalls fondly how they all had a love for water and sports and would go swimming to Merlin Club every Sunday.

The more I heard from Hari Prasad's friends, the more I realized what makes Hari, Hari. There are people who will say anything to please you, who will talk so much more than they will ever be of help—people who will judge, back-bite, turn their backs. Hari is the exact opposite. Without saying much or making a big deal out of it, he is always there for his friends. He never lets money, or what he has become in life, come in the way of deep friendships. He believes in being there—through good times and bad times, and all his friends feel they can rely on him. Further, Hari Prasad Kanoria is great company—always happy, calm and composed; someone who derives as much joy out of making others eat and enjoy life as does himself. All in all, if you have had the opportunity to have Hari Prasad Kanoria as a friend, you know, innately, this one is for keeps.

Chapter 22

My Friend Sancheti

Some friendships for Hari began as a professional relationship, grew into a close personal one and then even went beyond. I.C. Sancheti's friendship could be counted as one of those.

He was Kedarnath's lawyer. It was he who introduced his son to Sancheti, saying, 'Please can you teach everything about income tax to my Hari? Hari will deal with all the income tax files henceforth.' Sancheti had the highest regard for Kedarnath and could not refuse. He told Hari jestingly, 'I will do all the helping, you do all the working!'

In Hari, Sancheti saw a promising young person who had the potential to do something very significant with his life. In all the circles, business or personal, that Sancheti had a foot in, he included Hari as he observed that Hari had the ability to touch anything and make it even more wonderful than it was. Sancheti would recommend Hari's name to every group, business community or chamber that he could. So much so that there came a time when wherever Sancheti's name figured, very naturally Hari Prasad Kanoria's name too would figure.

The relationship between the two blossomed so much that they became more like family friends and would ask each other for advice in all matters, be it financial or relationships, ideas or decisions.

Sancheti beautifully sums up his relationship with Hari. He says, what he has learnt from Hari is this:

1) Competence: Finish all the work you start; never leave anything midway. Whatever was assigned to Hari would

inevitably be completed.

2) Humility: Even though I am younger than him, he puts my convenience first. The meetings of our Trust could easily have been conducted at his residence, but he always insisted that he would come to my house instead.

3) Altruism: His mantra is, 'One should possess the ability and capacity to contribute to the family, society, country and world.'

4) Be family-oriented: He has always insisted that family interests be prioritized. This resulted in the concept of 'Sunday is my family day.'

5) Be Adjusting: We both are very different as people. He believes in dharm gurus and I believe in science. Yet, we have never had a fight (they have now known each other for close to 60 years). Sometimes he adjusts to my view, at other times I do. We do it so naturally, without even needing to speak or discuss.

Great relationships are the manna of life. Hari Prasad Kanoria was indeed blessed, from a very young age, to find many of them. Moreover, he made it a point to be a great friend to many.

From left to right: I.C. Sancheti; K.C. Agarwal; Hari Prasad Kanoria; Jagjivan Ram, the then Defence Minister, Government of India; and N.K. Jalan. April 1978 at the Calcutta Chamber of Commerce.

Chapter 23

The Circle of Life

In the 1960s, often when a matter of great sensitivity had to be communicated to someone close to you, the help of a go-between was taken. Kedarnath knew it was time for his eldest son to get married, but seeing Hari's zeal for the business and his education, he knew if he broached the subject, he would come to a dead end.

Kedarnath Kanoria was a wise man. He sought the advice and counsel of one of his very close friends who was the chief justice of the Calcutta High Court. He mentioned his issue to him, and the friend happily took on the challenge of convincing Hari for matrimony.

One day, casually, over a cup of evening tea he said to Hari, 'Beta, your father is now forty and you are twenty. When he was twenty, he had you. There is always a time and space for everything and this is the right time for you to get married. Your father is not too young and not too old, and will enjoy his grandchildren. In any case, he is training you in the skill of business whilst you are doing graduation and law.'

Hari was slightly taken aback.

He was at that phase in life when everything was fluid. After graduation he was now studying to become an advocate. Law was not just a subject but a passion, and his mind, so sharp, so analytical, was being challenged to its fullest at Law College. Along with his studies he was also learning the ropes at business. At such a stage did it make sense to tie oneself down to a lifetime of responsibility? He wasn't sure.

Hari's grandmother and mother too had been trying to persuade him to marry, citing the examples of both uncles and other cousins, but he had stood his ground. However, Hari trusted the advice of some people. The chief justice's words made sense to Hari. He could see clearly the lives of some people—how doing the right thing at the right time had helped them rise high in the personal and professional spheres. After some resistance, and hesitation, he decided to follow what 'Uncle', the chief justice, was saying.

Hari couldn't think as far as great-grandchildren or grandchildren playing in the lap of his grandmother, father and mother but he trusted the flow of life and said yes, but on one condition: He should be allowed to study and focus on his work. He would take utmost care of his wife, as he had always seen the Kanoria men treat their women with great love and respect, but he should be allowed to continue his quest for professional growth. Marriage should complement him, not be in competition with everything he wanted to achieve.

Kedarnath was all too ready.

And that is how Hari, the happy, carefree, boisterous, and passionate young lad got ready to transform himself for the next stage of his life: Grihastha Ashram.

Hari the bridegroom

Wedding bells—Hari and Champa Devi

Chapter 24

A Partnership for Life

Nathuram Poddar was considered a famous, well-loved and well-respected person in Calcutta those days. He had many daughters (shy of a cricket team!) and one among them, his sixth daughter, Champa Devi, was recommended for Hari.

The Poddars and the Kanorias were seen to be on equal footing, be it in reputation or in culture, in business or spirituality, hence a common acquaintance suggested that the two youngsters from the families should be married.

Their horoscopes were matched, and it seemed to suggest that a lifetime of abundance was assured by this divine match. So Hari was taken to meet Champa Devi. As soon as he saw her—with her almond eyes, beautiful Indian skin, long hair and the way she was conducting herself with grace and poise, he was sure that she would be his partner for a lifetime—the woman who would be his strength, his inner voice, the wind beneath his wings.

On 10 March 1961, their sacred union took place amidst much pomp and show, love and laughter. Hari had found his most beneficial, long-term and rewarding companionship till date.

Whenever I see Hari Prasad and Champa Devi together, I can't help but smile. They complement each other perfectly. He is loud, she is soft. He is tough, she is tender. He is a businessman, she an ardent seeker. The two of them look at each other with so much love. I have watched as long conversations flow between them. Be it about a get-together or about a child, they converse like best friends.

Every morning she wakes up, dresses in the finest of saris, wears jewellery and adorns her hair with flowers—she believes it is her responsibility to always be beautiful for her God as well as her husband. The two of them will be arguing in the cutest manner and he will suddenly burst out laughing as she starts getting angry for real. It has been a delight to watch the two of them relate to one another. While they appear polar opposites, I think in reality they are like two shores with a river flowing in between—the shores look apart, but when you go to the bed of the river, the depths, there are no two shores. There exists just one flow...

Hari and Champa Devi at the Taj Mahal

The young couple

Chapter 25

Breaking Norms

As we have seen, from a very early age, Hari loved challenging norms.

A legend clearly doesn't follow others' paths—he creates them. And Hari often did that.

Freshly married, he was often invited by his mother-in-law for dinner. Champa Devi had seven sisters and Hari would be welcomed with great fanfare as the sixth son-in-law.

One would expect that to impress all his in-laws—the members of the family eagerly watching every move, every gesture to see what kind of new specimen had been added to the family— Hari would wear his smartest shirt and pant (add that suit, just to be safe). But no, not our Hari. Instead, he would take his patriotic feelings to his in-laws' home by wearing a simple kurta and dhoti, like a simple village folk. He liked to display the rustic life and his roots—and his mother-in-law would often laugh and tease him, saying, 'Hari is such a simpleton.' Hari would join in the laughter, and on his next visit he would once again don clothes that would cause much mirth. His mother-in-law would say to him that he would become a neta (leader) one day.

Also, being a lady belonging to a bygone era of orthodox India, his mother-in-law kept a 'ghoonghat', which basically meant that the loose end of her sari was worn over the head in a way that it hid almost half her face. At that time, a married woman were not supposed to show her face to men, other than her father, husband and son.

Whenever Hari visited his in-laws' house, he would lift the

barrier between his mother-in-law and him. When she resisted, he would happily tell her, 'You call me your son, right? Then why this ghoonghat between us? I want you to be comfortable and informal with me.' This would earn him peals of laughter from eight women in the house and, I am sure, respect too. For no one in that era really dared question the prevalent social practices.

To most people, what was, was. It was obviously not so for Hari.

To cite an example of Hari being his own man, he was going to Victoria Gardens from his in-laws' home. His father-in-law had this firm belief that no outside food should be consumed as it was unhealthy and unhygienic. He was quite strict, and his word was pretty much the law at home. As Hari prepared to leave, his father-in-law said, 'Son, don't eat any snacks—like cold drinks or phuchka (a popular street food) sold on the road. Outside food is not good for us.' To this Hari, an ardent phuchka-lover, immediately responded, saying, 'Father, I will not have outside food, but phuchka is okay. It is not outside food. In fact, you should have it too!'

I could literally visualize the scene as he spoke about this. Both Manisha and I burst out laughing. We could picture Hari's father-in-law taking that first bite of outside food, with Hari convincing him, 'This is not outside food—eat, eat.' Indeed, to be Hari was something else.

Chapter 26

Brain and Sandesh

Marriage comes with its own sweets and savouries. Literally. Mothers-in-law are born to pamper their sons-in-law and Champa Devi's mother took her role very seriously. Every now and then carloads of sweetmeats and salty snacks would be sent to the Kanoria home. Sandesh, a Bengali sweet, was fast becoming a weakness for Hari. He would literally have 10-20 sandesh in a day.

Legends are nothing, if not eccentric.

In those days the famous lawyer, Chittaranjan Das ate almost one or two kilos of sandesh every day. Whether it was to justify Hari's own sandesh consumption or simply create an atmosphere of fun as they all devoured the sandesh, Hari would say out loud, 'If we eat sandesh, we will also become as intelligent as Chittaranjan Das! Now isn't that a great reason to consume more sandesh and remain—guilt free at the same time?' Despite eating the quantity of sandesh that he did, he maintained his weight between 70 to 72 kg as he had deeply internalized the value of good health, ensuring that abundance of food came with abundance of exercise.

Every evening along with glasses full of frothy, creamy milk, sandesh would be laid out for everyone. All the members in the house were only too ready to eat it. Apart from the *sandesh*, he consumed no sugar and no sugary drinks.

We shall never know if all that sandesh resulted in rising levels of intelligence in the Kanoria family, but I am guessing it certainly played its part in adding to the cute little pot belly that Hari Prasad sports even today.

Chapter 27

What's in a Name?

When I asked Hari about the happiest moment in his life, he didn't blink for a second. He didn't have to. It was without doubt the moment when his firstborn, Hemant, was born, in August 1962. Holding the little bundle of joy in his arms, Hari felt he was the luckiest man on earth. He also recognized what his grandfather and father would have felt when he was born. He experienced this feeling five times—when one after the other—Hari and Champa Devi became the proud parents of four sons and finally a daughter.

When Hemant was born, Hari's grandmother, mother and father wanted to keep his name Bishambar. Bishambar signifies Lord Shiva, the Lord of the Universe. Everybody called him Bishambar as he was born in the month of August, right at the time of a Shivaratri.

Champa Devi was not happy with the name. Influenced by her young, modern-minded sisters, she felt the name was a bit too heavy-sounding and old-fashioned for a handsome boy like theirs. Hari was adamant that Bishambar was just fine—in fact, everyone had already taken to it. The couple often lovingly argued about the name. Meanwhile, his birth certificate, official papers of importance and many other papers continued to have the name Bishambar. At his first school, Nopany High School, and in the next, the child answered to the name Bishambar.

However, Champa persisted, like a gentle river cutting through the rock. Finally Hari surrendered: if it meant so much to his wife, why not? When the boy was admitted to the Hindi

High School, his name was changed to Hemant. Not that it made any difference to him, but since it brought so much joy to his mother, Hemant happily reconciled to his new identity.

Patterns have a strange way of repeating themselves. Every single child born to Hari and Champa Devi was named and renamed. Their second son Sanjeev (born in September 1963) was named Purshottam—once again the name of a God, this time, Lord Vishnu. Once again Champa Devi felt it wasn't contemporary enough—so Purshottam became Sanjeev.

Their third son was born in May 1965 and was named Damodar (a name for Krishna) by the elders including Hari. Soon enough Champa Devi changed it to Sunil. She was adamant—Hemant and Sanjeev were such wonderful names. To have a third one called Damodar wouldn't do at all. Hari knew better than to argue. Partly exasperated and partly amused, he agreed, wondering what else life had in store for them as far as names went.

The last of their sons was born (April 1968) during the time of Basant so Hari wondered if it was okay to call him that. Champa Devi didn't immediately reply but in a few days she said, 'My brother's name is Basant. How can my brother and son have the exact same name?' Hari replied with exaggerated patience, 'My dear wife, your brother is Basant Poddar, our son is Basant Kanoria. Where is the confusion?'

Champa Devi did not look happy or convinced—so the last of their four sons was renamed Sujit. The beauty of it was that the children continued to be called by their original names—Bishambar, Purshottam, Damodar and Basant—at home by all the family members except Champa Devi. Hari would often tease her that she was being as insolent as Ma Sati was towards Lord Shiva! (According to mythology, Ma Sati went to her parents' home despite Lord Shiva warning her that it would not be good to do so.)

After four boys the couple craved for a dash of pink amidst all the blue, a little girl with soft hands and feet and a gentle smile, among four big, boisterous boys. Desire with all your heart and it shall happen, was the motto of Hari. And he wasn't willing to give up on his dream of having a little angel in their home.

Finally she came—with a wail, putting a smile on everyone's faces. Hemlata (born in December 1971), the little girl with big cheeks, huge eyes and a smile that could melt any heart, was Daddy's little girl, the answer to a mother's longing, and the favourite of the four brothers who couldn't fathom how the dark-eyed baby would change their world.

It seemed as if she would be an exception to the renaming game, for Hemlata was liked by the proud father and mother, and especially loved by Hemant who felt she was his little flower. But some things are just not meant to be. When the family visited the beautiful Mansa Devi temple in Haridwar everybody unanimously decided that Hemlata would become Manisha. Manisha, indifferent to the goings-on, happily looked at her family and wondered, what's in a name anyway?

Hemant & Sanjeev

Sanjeev & Sunil

Sujit

Manisha

Chapter 28

The Fine Balance

*G*rihastha ashram is all about finding the fine balance between the chaotic family scene and the demanding work front, between family and employees, and between love and opportunities for growth. The important thing is to not lose focus—that is, give of oneself so much to one role that the other suffers.

Hari somehow managed to get the balance beautifully right.

He was very clear that the children were his priority. They were his world and he was responsible to God for nurturing them. While he was a law student, he would give adequate time to Bishambhar, alias Hemant and Purshottam, alias Sanjeev. He would cradle them in his arms while holding a book.

When he came back home from work late and they happened to be studying, he would take each one of them, make them sit in his lap and talk to them about the happenings of their day. He would almost be like a mother to them when any one of them fell ill or got hurt, nurturing them back to health and happiness with his tender words and a big box of homeopathic medicines. He also took it upon himself to flood their lives with inspiration, be it in the form of movies, music, books or sports.

He ensured his children were taught Vedic stories and the teachings of Swami Vivekananda. The family would go for movies on weekends and he would take them to watch classics like *The Sound of Music Mary Poppins* as well as *Charlie Chaplin* movies to open their minds not just to Indian cinema but also Hollywood. He ensured that they had the best of books from across the world to read. In fact, he started a library so that his children could indulge in as much reading as possible.

He would also take the kids to the Ordnance Club for a swim. He wanted them to imbibe the values of Swami Vivekananda which pretty much governed his life: develop muscles of iron, nerves of steel and a mind like a thunderbolt. He encouraged them to play sports before reading the Gita because he believed that one's body is one's first temple. He was fond of telling them, 'Health is Wealth' and that it is in a healthy body that a healthy mind resides.

As the kids developed healthy bodies and able minds, Hari's chest would swell with pride on seeing them; he considered them to be his greatest treasure. In fact, they even exhibited an entrepreneurial-cum-social spirit from a very young age when they started a library at home in 1971, calling it the Sri Krishna Library. They would loan their books—to family, friends and others, charging fifty paise a book for a week!

On the professional front, Hari had completed his education. After obtaining a law degree from Calcutta University he had enrolled as an advocate at the Calcutta High Court and the Bar Council of West Bengal. While he had been groomed from a young age to observe and participate in his father and grandfather's business enterprises, as a mature individual, with a strong knowledge of law and driven by a vibrant entrepreneurial spirit, decided to fully embrace the legacy of running the family enterprise as persuaded by his father.

Hari began his career in managing the family manufacturing and trading business. After raising them to greater heights of success, he also started the manufacturing of stainless steel and aluminium utensils in Patna.

If Hari knew how to be soft with his family, he also knew how to be fearlessly confrontational when the situation called for it. He talks about the time when the state government was not giving him clearances for the factory in Patna for manufacturing stainless steel and aluminum utensils, which made it very difficult for him to get a supply of raw material. After struggling for months, Hari finally went to the state industry minister and told him in a voice filled with awe-inspiring authority for a man that young, 'Sir, businessmen are not treated properly in Bihar. No one should come here with dreams of expansion. You and your predecessors have been coming to Calcutta and inviting businessmen to invest in Bihar. But once they are here, they are used as scapegoats.'

The government official stared at the fiery young man before him and was taken aback by his words. He said to him, 'You say you are from Barhiya and your mannerisms are that of Biharis too. Then why are you saying such things? You should encourage businessmen to come to your native land and help it grow!'

To this Hari immediately replied, 'Sir, I don't wish to offend you, but look at my own condition. I started this factory to provide employment and quality products, but I have not been given the clearances for two years now and it is making life hell for me. In such a situation, how do you expect me to recommend businessmen to come to Bihar?'

The message was well heard and well received. Within a few days, Hari received the clearances for his factory.

Chapter 29

Education Unfolds Potential

In the Kanoria home, education had been always considered to be of prime importance.

But it was not just about school and college, desks and chairs, chalk and board—the Kanorias believed that more than anything else, it was what they learnt from examples at home and the workplace that would leave a lifelong imprint.

Hari had learnt so much by being close to his grandfather and father. Be it managing people or managing emotions, accounting for money or accounting for situations—these couldn't be taught in the classroom. These were subjects learnt from life, taught by life.

To ensure that his children experienced the best of life's education, Hari asked them all to come to their office and study. In any case, with four growing boys and one little girl, an extended family, guests and chores, Champa Devi had her hands more than full. She couldn't wait for her gang to be with their father for a while, so that she could find time to remember who she was. The siblings would fight so much that the perfect antidote was to send them off to the office where, in the presence of their father, grandfather and uncles, a semblance of peace would be maintained.

The children were promptly made to pack their books after school and study in the office. The 'study' was of a different kind, Hari made sure of that. While their books were opened—and pencils were sharpened for homework—he also made it a point to open their hearts and sharpen their minds. He purposely had business-related conversations before the children so that they could see how he thought, how he spoke and how he took decisions.

Sometimes the children observed strategies being developed, and at other times they observed deals being sealed; sometimes they were privy to complex conversations as well as peaceful resolutions, and at other times they watched how money was being handled. All of this taught the children so much about their father, what he did and how he did it.

Often after a conversation with someone, Hari would ask the children for their opinions or thoughts. This would help them to come up with ideas on business when they were barely in their teens, and it began to fine-tune their minds towards aspects that most probably would not have been covered in the curriculum.

Not just from their father, the children learnt a lot from the staff as well. They will always fondly remember a senior Bengali gentleman, Jyotirmoy Roy, or Roy Babu, who taught the children much about the mannerisms of Bengalis, as well as the language. This helped them immensely in the years to come, especially on how to conduct themselves with officials and politicians. He was 70 years old, a great friend of Hari's father and a good counsellor for Hari in all matters.

It is not enough for a tree to grow. It has to drop seeds to ensure more trees can grow, and eventually become a forest.

That's exactly what Hari was doing.

I couldn't help it. As I listened, I visualized a young Megha along with the five children, sitting in their office and listening to Hari Prasad's conversations—sharing ideas, giving inputs. If I had had that opportunity, I am sure my poet-writer's mind would have known a lot more about numbers and business too.

Nevertheless, I am not dejected, or disappointed. Rather, as I watch Hari Prasad take a small break to sign some cheques and talk to his accountant, I feel excited. Perhaps before this book ends, I would have had the opportunity to overhear enough conversations for it to activate my latent business capabilities. Now that's a fringe benefit I didn't anticipate, but it is more than welcome.

Chapter 30

Let Them Fight

The state sports minister was a friend of Hari's. He would often send the family VIP tickets for various matches. Hari would happily take all the children and sit right in front where he could not only enjoy the game, but also take the opportunity of teaching his kids invaluable lessons about the various excursions.

Hari and his sons thoroughly enjoyed wrestling matches. There were famous wrestlers like Dara Singh, Randhawa and King Kong and the five of them would sit in the first row watching every move with complete fascination.

The fights didn't end in the wrestling courts. The boys would try every move at home. Hands, legs, teeth—everything was be put to use as they emulated every move, much to poor Champa Devi's anguish! The boys would break glass, bottles and pretty much everything that was breakable at home, except each other's neck. Champa Devi would come rushing to Hari and say, 'See what your sons are up to.' And Hari would say, 'Let them fight— they will learn so much by fighting.' Before Champa Devi could reply, Hari would quickly get out of the way. He never stopped the fights among the children, so they would become stronger and smarter. After saying this, he would go into hiding to escape the wrath of his wife.

Manisha was the favourite plaything of all the brothers. She was an easy target, soft and sweet, cute and cuddly, and they would use her as their punching bag sometimes. As long as the four boys fought amongst each other, Champa Devi would contain herself—and accept her fate with some mumbling and grumbling. However, the moment her darling daughter was involved and came crying to her for help, Champa Devi would become an avatar of Ma Kali. (Manisha had learnt early enough—as long as it was fun for her, she would let her brothers do what they wanted. The moment it went beyond her limit, off she would run to her mother to complain.) Champa Devi would twist the boys' arms and beat them up. The most notorious and adventurous among them was Sanjeev.

Being with her brothers, Manisha learnt the ropes fast enough. She knew she could not beat them in might, so she didn't even bother. Instead, she would use tears, words and other tricks up her sleeve to get back at the fantastic and furious four.

One day Sujit, the one closest to her in age, was troubling her beyond belief. They were playing outside their dad's office, and he was hassling her. Manisha hatched a plan. She chewed a paan, which stained her mouth red. It looked like blood. Off went Manisha with her 'wounded' mouth and complained that Sujit had done it. Sujit received a pounding from Hari. Manisha knew that she had special powers and could get anyone in trouble, in a jiffy.

As Hari Prasad recalled all these heartwarming incidents about his children' growing-up years, he would suddenly start chuckling. Sometimes he would remain lost, in a gossamer of nostalgia, and I would watch a gentle smile blossom on his lips. It was unusual to see a business icon look so blissful and peaceful as he recalled those little moments from his past.

Chapter 31

Bande Mataram and Rasgulla

The 1970s were daunting times in eastern India. The streets spilled over with social unrest and political discontent, and businesses were rushing out of Calcutta because of insufficient governance and unionized labour, which led to frequent strikes—in short, it was a terrible time for starting or expanding a business.

But the Kanorias were known for their ability to see opportunity even in times of crisis. After all, from the times of their forefathers they had been accustomed to dealing with tough times—not just surviving but conquering every adversity and turning it to their advantage.

In late 1969, Kedarnath purchased the prestigious Bengal Flour Mills Co. Ltd from Balmer Lawrie as a joint family business with two uncles and two brothers. It was a publicly listed blue chip company and Asia's largest flour mill at that time. In Hari, Kedarnath saw a capable man gifted with the knowledge of managing people and calamities, and as someone who had a strong hold over law. He entrusted Hari with the responsibility of turning the struggling company around despite the economic, political and social barriers that the industry was facing.

Hari loved challenges. If there was one passion he had, it was to take a concern which was not doing well and convert it into a success story. With faith in himself, in his father's decision and in God, he put all his energy into steering the flour mill.

Within two months of their takeover of the flour mill, there was a strike by the security personnel and workmen. Hari took the setback in his stride and, with the aid of a few loyal workmen and some government (then Congress) help, continued running the mill even during the strike. He used his intelligence to understand that a few people were causing the unrest and he dismissed them so peace could be retained. A wonderful attribute of Hari was his concern for their welfare—he continued to pay them compensation for two years but did not take them back in employment.

After a few years, a union leader along with workmen tried to bully Hari by placing a revolver on the table. In a voice that spoke of peace and righteousness, Hari said, 'Kill me if you wish, but I will only give what is rightfully due to you. I will not get pressured by you under any circumstances. I know I have done the right thing, you may do as you please.' Needless to say, when such power and strength emanates from the soul, there is no option but to relent and so did the striking workers.

There were many issues that came up—from everywhere, acting as hindrances to the work that went on in the mill. In one of the factories, the agreement was with a union affiliated to the political party which was in power, namely the Communist Party of India (Marxist). After the All India Trinamool Congress (TMC) came into power, all the workers joined the union affiliated to TMC. They conveniently stated that they would now no longer follow the existing agreement on wage revision, even though it had been signed just three months ago. They demanded a hike in salary which Hari plainly refused. It was sheer bullying and Hari had learnt long back that when faced with a bully, you have to fight back and bully him.

During that time as Hari was on his way out of his mill, the labourers surrounded his car and refused to let him leave. They kept raising slogans asking for justice. Hari was clear he had done nothing wrong—and was paying wages as per the agreement. He wasn't one to fall for such intimidation.

Meanwhile, the anger of the mob was rising and Hari's executives urged him to call the police for help. Hari refused.

He saw his labourers as his people—his family at the workplace. The solution was not to use might but to allow them to let off steam and then talk to them.

Any other person in such a situation would have got nervous. Just visualize it—a car with just the driver and Hari in it, surrounded by a mob of workers screaming at the top of their lungs. Things could have gone any which way. Not with Hari, though. His strength came from the conviction of being right. He knew he was a good employer and hence fear did not touch him.

After about one-and-a-half hours of staying in the car, during which time Hari happily read a book even as the mob kept trying to get a reaction out of him, they finally started shouting, '*Bande Mataram, Bande Mataram.*' That was when Hari got out of the car and screamed, '*Bande Mataram, Bande Mataram! Kaam karna padega, kaam karoge to dal roti milega, rasgulla nahi!* (there's no way other than work; if you work you will earn your daily bread, not rasgulla).'

The workers didn't know how to respond to someone like Hari who never lost his temper and was just not willing to budge. By and by, they resumed work and the day's calm and order was regained.

These are just a few among the numerous challenges faced by Hari. Whatever be the issue, it was with an attitude of remarkable cool and courage that every challenge was addressed.

As Hari Prasad was describing the incident at the mill I felt I was pretty much a part of a Bollywood film. I could visualize the workers in their blue overalls screaming at Hari Prasad in his suit, no less than a superstar with his original lines. However, the beauty of life is that there no re-takes, you get only one chance to get it right. A decision can go any which way. What matters is to stay true to your values, and yourself. I think this is exactly what Hari Prasad managed to do time and time again.

Chapter 32

Do Not Invite Me

If there was one quality in Hari that made him grow, it was his people skills. He was large-hearted and jovial, enterprising and straightforward, and anyone who met Hari wanted to be associated with him in some form or the other. These social skills made him a much sought after figure and he was invited to be a part of several chambers of commerce, associations and societies in the eastern region as well as the national level. Very soon, with his acumen and industry leadership qualities, he became the president of The Calcutta Trades Association in 1976. It was established as early as 1830 and to be its president was considered quite prestigious among businessmen and industrialists.

At that time, Jagjivan Ram was the deputy prime minister. He was known to Hari through his father. Hari wanted to increase the influence of the Association, so he invited him for a function. He felt it would add to the stature of the group and all its members. Jagjivan Ram replied warmly but frankly, 'Beta, please do not invite me to such small places and gatherings. Do something significant, transform it into a big chamber and then I will readily come. I shall not immediately say yes because I know my refusal will only help you to expand the organization...'

Hari, as always, loved challenges. He said, 'I will definitely do this, Sir, and then I will come back to you. You will happily accept my invitation then, I am sure.'

He discussed the matter with his friends at the Association and told them that they needed to expand its scope of work—and it had to begin with the name. He suggested changing the name of the Association to Calcutta Chamber of Commerce. His friends and contemporaries were quite resistant. They said, how can we change the name in time for the function?

Being a law graduate was always of great help to Hari. He knew what the law said and this gave him a great edge in various situations. He immediately said, 'It can be changed by the registrar of companies.'

The regional head was one Mr Mullick and he dismissed Hari almost outright, saying, 'Mr Kanoria, you have to file the papers for such things. For almost twenty years, no papers have been filed by the Association hence this does not look possible.'

Hari was not willing to give up. In fact, the word give up did not exist in his dictionary so he told his friends that they needed to somehow collect all the papers and do the needful. Some of them said a clear no and were unwilling to help in any way. It did not daunt Hari. Once he had decided on something, nothing could stop him. He managed to put the documents together within a few days and the Association's name was changed to the Calcutta Chamber of Commerce. He also managed to change the logo, expand the Chamber's scope of work and revamp the organization completely.

Within two months, right before the function, Hari visited Jagjivan Ram with a newfound confidence, a brand new outlook and an organization that seemed to have grown into something much bigger than it was before.

Jagjivan Ram couldn't help but say yes.

And for Hari, the episode couldn't help but deepen his faith: When you really want something—and when that something is for the higher good—the whole universe conspires to make it happen.

It's one thing to have read this nugget of wisdom in Paulo Coelho's famous book, *The Alchemist*, it's completely different to see this truth unfold before your eyes. In so many situations I have seen Hari Prasad's life stand testimony to this truth, and it reaffirmed my faith time and time again, that nothing is impossible.

Dr Hari Prasad Kanoria with Shri Jagjivan Ram, Hon'ble Defence Minister, GoI on 30 April 1978

Left to Right: Hari, I. C. Sancheti, N. K. Jalan with Shri Pranab Mukherjee at the Calcutta Chamber of Commerce, 1973

Chapter 33
Face the Brutes

An onslaught of challenges seemed to pick on Hari in the mid-1980s. They came from everywhere. At home things were beginning to get bad as the brothers began to face issues after their mother's demise on 20 June 1980.

It is said that when a pure soul drenched in the love of God leaves its earthly body, calamities start visiting the family. Hari's mother would divide the earnings of the family among the brothers based on the number of children each of them had. However, after her passing, it was decided that all the money would be divided among Hari's father, Hari and his two brothers in four equal shares.

Hari had more children. He wanted that all the children, while living in a joint family, should live and enjoy the family fortune equally. There must not be any inequality. Hari felt strongly that his father ought to have dealt with an iron fist as Swami Vivekananda would do while dealing with difficult situations. Unfortunately, due to the shock of his wife's demise, Kedarnath had become a silent spectator. He could not command the family members as his wife had done.

Hari asked his father to give him his one-fourth share or some money to start his own business. He clarified that he would continue to work for the family business too. But he was compelled to have his own kitchen despite living in a joint family. Hari's family members also started asking him to resign from his role as the secretary/CEO of the Bengal Flour Mills, as they felt his role was nominal. They said they were willing to give him money if he would resign, but if he continued in the position, he would just be a nominal head—with no power or money.

That did not feel right to Hari. He had given his sweat and blood to the mills despite all odds and the business was rightfully as much his as anyone else's in the family. Even his father-in-law and wife urged him to relinquish that namesake position and accept the money, but Hari didn't budge.

He had this inexplicable belief that he would be able to navigate his ship through the fiercest of storms. Though everything in the world outside looked unforgiving and challenging, the world within him remained strong—a bastion of trust and faith.

In fact, in 1981, by God's grace he got the opportunity to take over two more flour mills, and Hemant, who was just eighteen years and studying, was already being groomed to assist Hari and revive the units under his able guidance.

Hari was convinced that his resignation from the Bengal Flour Mills would show his weakness, people might think that the family had forced him to resign due to questionable activities. His name and fame would be affected.

While he was reluctant to give up his nominal position in the family business, he was clear that he had to build his own fortune. In one of the flour mills located in Kolkata, the Sri Radha Krishna Flour Mills (Pvt) Ltd, they had some major problems with the land owner. Taking it upon himself, with unparalleled acumen coupled with intuition, he was able to resolve the problem. With the able advice of renowned lawyer and Congress leader Ajit Panja, Hari won the case. Normalcy was restored.

The other flour mill was in Krishnanagar, twenty-five km from Mayapur, near the Iskcon headquarters. Hari named it Chaitanya Flour Mills. That area was the birthplace of Chaitanya Mahaprabhu, the great Viashnava saint.

Behind the mill was a colony called Shaktinagar which was controlled by Naxalites. An influential and infamous Naxal leader, known for his ruthless behaviour—he was someone who could go to any extent to get what he wanted—requested Hari to employ more than fifty people from his group in the mill. Hari refused. To get back at him the Naxalites closed the factory by force.

At that time, Hari had perishable goods valued at about Rs 7 crore within the mill. If they were not recovered, his investment would be lost. Nobody would cover the loss, saying it was due to external factors.

His advisor then was Jyotirmay Roy, or Roy Babu, who was a friend of his father. Hari was very close to him. A man of wisdom and integrity, he was highly educated. He had resigned from the post of magistrate and was associated with Kedarnath. Despite the displeasure within his family, he chose to work with Hari, foregoing the compensation which he had been getting from his family. Moreover, he worked with Hari without any compensation. Hari was indebted to him. Roy Babu also groomed Hemant and Sanjeev to handle seemingly impossible situations.

The Naxalites had put flags all over and were not allowing them to enter. In response, Hari and Roy Babu approached the district magistrate and police officials explaining that they had been barred from entering into their own premises. The authorities said that unless some law was broken, nothing could be done—as it was a labour dispute.

So, Hari, in consultation with Roy Babu, arranged for trucks and other workers and made his way to the factory. As they entered the factory, the Naxals tried to create a commotion. Immediately, Hari called the police which had to act to restore law and order. With protection, Hari was able to retrieve all the perishable goods. Within fifteen days, the workers surrendered, realizing that it was in their best interests to get back to work as Hari was not showing any signs of budging. Peace was restored, work was started. Hari said with a great sigh of relief that he had drawn courage from Swami Vivekananda's words—'Face the brutes'—and the message of Lord Krishna to Arjuna.

There were two important insights that I received from this particular incident in Hari Prasad's life. The first was that it takes some courage to go against unrighteous people who are against you. But it takes an altogether different level of courage to stand up to the people you love and respect. Hari held on to his position at the Bengal Flour Mills despite his own father-in-law and wife urging him against it because he knew he was in the right. He was willing to stand for what was right even under extreme pressure.

The second insight was that the challenges are never-ending; so are the great times. It's kind of like playing a video game. When you pass one level, you are taken to a higher level of difficulty. The thrill of playing this level is greater too. For any person, life will always be a beautiful series of snakes and ladders—one without the other actually makes no sense.

Chapter 34

Me' vs 'We'

The year 1980 was probably one of the most challenging ones for Hari. It was the year his mother passed away. His mother was like that invisible string that held the entire family together. Seemingly simple, innocuous—and yet everything seemed to be in place because of her. Her presence was enough to keep the entire family together, and with her passing, everything fell into a state of chaos.

There was rivalry amongst the brothers. Everyone wanted a space for themselves. There were conflicts in the business, and the thinking was, more 'me' than 'we'. Living together, working together and praying together seemed to have become a challenge as each one tried to somehow cope with losing the anchor that had tied the boat of their relationships onshore. Things seemed to be disintegrating beyond repair.

Hari's father too had an emotional setback for a while upon losing his wife. The usually mild and always-in-control person was at a loss to know what to do—it was his way of coping with the loss of six decades of impeccable companionship. He had been in command, managing the larger family of three branches and his own two brothers from the time of his father's demise in 1955.

For Hari, it was probably most difficult as he didn't know how to keep the flock together and also keep his father happy. The struggles on the business front were growing too—the uncles and brothers wanted Hari to be out of the family's joint business.

From Basant Panchami in 1981, Hari started his own trading and supply business. With a wife, five children studying and squabbling siblings, life seemed to be hanging precariously on the brink of uncertainty.

It was during this time that Hari retreated for a couple of days to Barhiya, to take stock of the land and home. It was also an attempt to give himself a breather so that he could clear his head and think things through.

He sat at a desk in front of the photo of Ma Kali (of the Dakshineswar Temple) at his home one afternoon, writing something and thinking to himself about what he would do ahead, with no money and so many responsibilities to execute, when suddenly he had a divine glimpse. He felt Ma Kali appear before him and say, 'My child, fret not for I am with you. Keep working—I will take care of the rest!'

He also felt that Mother was telling him that there were so many poor people in the world in need of employment and work. He had to think of the larger picture and work in full consciousness of Mother Divine. She seemed to be saying to him, 'You are in a much better position than them, you must rise yourself and uplift them.'

This one spiritual intervention changed the entire course of Hari's life. It filled him with a new-found faith and vigour. It made him excited about the future rather than worry about it. It made him feel responsible, not sorry. It changed everything—in an instant as moments like these usually do. Much like a streak of lightning across a dark, sleepy city which lights it up for a moment, Hari's life underwent a complete transformation.

He remembered a few lines from *The Alchemist* to the effect that God opens a door for prosperity when calamities seize from all sides.

While nothing seemed to have changed in the world outside on that sleepy afternoon in Barhiya, nothing remained the same in the world within.

As Hari Prasad Kanoria was recalling this instance, I experienced something I had not until then. As he spoke, the room seemed still. And his voice wavered and quivered. Suddenly he burst into tears. It was not easy for me to see him break down like that. The man who had made me laugh all along now suddenly made his way into my heart with the purity of his tears and devotion. Devotion is the base on which the very foundation of his life, his relationships and business rests.

Hari seeking solace in prayer   Hari's mother: The passing of an era

Hari at the Ramakrishna Mission in Vrindavan.
The statue of Swami Vivekananda was installed by Hari.

Chapter 35
The Uprising

While struggling to run the flour mills of joint and personal nature, along with managing his trading and supply business, Hari was keen to start some new business. Hemant, who was only nineteen then, was already his right hand man. He was an important part of all decision making and Hari saw in him a reflection of himself (with a smile Hari Prasad Kanoria adds that the only difference between them is that his son is more intelligent). Sunil too was excited about their business prospects and was clear that he wanted to join his father and elder brother in all their endeavours.

Sujit who had been suffering from ill health for a while insisted that he wanted to go to the US for further studies. Hari was not at all keen to send him. He kept trying to distract him, telling him that since he wrote so well, he should write a book on spirituality.

Sujit, like Hari, was listening to his inner voice. The duo went to Vrindavan to meet one Pagla Baba to seek his blessings, which was always fruitful. Hari requested him to have a look at Sujit and asked when his health would revive. Pagla Baba said that in two or three years Sujit would regain his health and also travel abroad for studies. Sujit's happiness knew no bounds. Now that he had Pagla Baba's blessings, he knew that the cards he held were stronger. And, as predicted, he went to the College of Wooster, Ohio, to study computer science.

Sujit had a business mindset. While studying in the USA, he wrote a letter to Hari, 'Father, I can see a market for handicrafts here. Can we export them from India?' Simultaneously, a friend approached Hari with a proposal to start manufacturing textile goods, mainly in silk, which could be procured and made in Varanasi. Hari was told that there was a demand for such products in Germany and Japan.

After examining all the factors, Hari got a company, namely the Sri Radha Krishna Export and Import Ltd, incorporated in Delhi with his chartered accountant friend. That was how their export business started.

Meanwhile Sanjeev had received admission in a medical college. There is an interesting incident about a tug-of-war between a strong-willed father and a stronger-willed son. One fine day Sanjeev came home and complained that it took him around one and-a-half hours to reach his college by car. He expressed his ardent desire for a motorcycle. Hari's nonchalant response, was, 'Why should your time be wasted, Sanjeev? You can read all your books in the car. The journey will give you more study time. Look at me, I read while I am in a bus, tram or car.'

Sanjeev retreated—for about twenty-four hours. Then he came back and repeated his request with vehemence. Hari kept explaining to him that it was not good for their prestige and also that he had heard of so many motorcycle accidents that he was not comfortable with the idea. Sanjeev refused to give up.

Finally, when Hari had run out of all excuses—and patience—he purchased a motorcycle but with a sidecar attached to it. He felt it was his way of protecting his son. As soon as Sanjeev saw the side car he was filled with anger. He didn't say anything and took the motorcycle with the side car to college for about five days. On the sixth day he detached the sidecar, saying that it was slowing him down; he was reaching college in the same time as when driving the car. The whole purpose of having a motorcycle was defeated.

Hari realized that he had always wanted all his children to be independent thinkers and leaders in their own right and that is exactly what he had achieved. Arguing didn't make sense any more, so he did the next best thing. Since Sanjeev's college was close to his factory in Cossipore, every day he would send someone from office to check on him. That person would also carry lunch for him and ensure he ate on time. Hari felt a very beautiful, tender love towards his children and wanted the best for them, under every circumstance.

Manisha, the apple of Hari's eye, was fascinated with children and wanted to get into the field of education. She did her Montessori training from London.

Family-work balance was the flavour of the decade for Hari—managing the growing needs of all his children, protecting their independence and yet ensuring they did not get hurt, dealing with the needs of an expanding business. There was so much to do.

Sanjeev's post-graduation from medical university in London. With Champa Devi, Hari and Sangeeta

Chapter 36

Your Company is Too Small

In the early 1990s, India was in a bad economic situation. Partition and wars, and political conflicts in the country, and decades of a virtually closed economy and red-tape had drained the economy. In 1992, when the then government of India opened up the economy, it knew that one of the most urgent steps needed for India to develop was to make infrastructure a prime sector.

Hari, a visionary from the start, could almost smell what was brewing in the government officials' minds and knew that infrastructure would be a key vertical that they should enter.

But infrastructure needs a lot of capital and they didn't have that at the time. What to do, what to do—the entrepreneur within Hari wrestled with the question.

Since he knew a few people in banks, he decided to approach them for a loan. He was told that he would need to apply for an infrastructure loan. The problem was that this kind of a loan was usually available to bigger players who had a reputation for being in construction. Hari continued to remain motivated. He realized that they would need to buy some of the large equipment needed if he wanted his application for the loan to be considered seriously. It was a strategy of the government to discourage small and medium companies—and work only with the big ones. They knew that the equipment was very expensive and none of the small fish could afford it. It was a catch 22—to apply for a loan, one needed equipment; and, to buy equipment, one needed a loan.

What would be the best approach, asked that voice in Hari's

head, which refused to give up.

He decided to approach all the banks he knew. He met a general manager who told him, 'Mr Kanoria, your company is so small—how can you get into infrastructure finance?' Hari replied, 'Sir whatever you give, I will accept happily. This is our vision and we want to see it through. It will help small and medium contractors in a big way. Their contributions will boost infrastructure projects.'

The general manager was willing to sanction a loan of Rs 5 lakh which was indeed a paltry sum. Still, Hari was not disheartened. He knew everyone had to begin somewhere. He told the general manager, 'Whatever be the amount, I will happily accept it as I want to start this journey with your good wishes. The bank official agreed and the loan was sanctioned.

Seeing one bank give a loan, a few more advanced loans, some small, some very small, but it gave Hari the confidence to begin. At that time both Hemant and Sunil were his trusted lieutenants and accompanied him everywhere. They watched with keen eyes and listened with eager ears, imbibing their father's never-say-die spirit.

It was in this humble way that SREI Finance began.

Sanjeev, Hemant and Sunil

Hemant and Sunil at the Srei office

Hemant Kanoria and Sunil Kanoria in the early years of SREI

Chapter 37

Small Will Become Big

Hari realized that if they had to make a mark in infrastructure, they would have to raise funds. Since banks were reluctant to lend them more money, they decided to go for a public issue. To grow, they needed the capital.

The approval for a public issue by a company needed to be secured from the government of India. Hari went to meet the government official concerned who was gentleman from Bihar. At the meeting, the officer addressed him as Sethji (a word used for affluent people) with a hint of sarcasm.

Hari immediately told him that he too hailed from Bihar. The official didn't look too impressed. He said that in the business that Hari was suggesting, the profits were too small for them to become a public listed company. Hari looked him straight in the eye and asked, 'Sir, do you want me to portray a large project and business plan with a large profit? The public will get excited and invest in me, but later, when they find out the truth, won't they lose faith in us? I will not do such a thing. I want to do things the genuine way.'

The official liked his spirit but stuck to his point. He said, 'I agree with everything, Sethji, but the fact is, the company and profits are too small to be listed.'

Hari argued, 'Small will become big. What did Dhirubhai Ambani start with? He was just a worker at a petrol pump. You will have to help me, Sir. I have confidence in our abilities. I am going to Vrindavan tomorrow. The day after, I shall come and take the approval from you.'

The official said nothing.

I was amazed as I heard about this incident. I immediately asked Hari Prasad Kanoria, how did you have so much confidence. He replied, 'I believe in myself. I believe in God. I knew our proposal was good. So what if we were small, we were a promising company. I had no doubts. I always move ahead with faith in self and faith in God.

Somehow I could feel that these were not just words. Rather, they came from someone who truly had no doubts about his intention and actions and hence life fuelled him with the energy to achieve his dreams. I have always doubted myself. Even when I know I have something good to offer, something in me has always been a little hesitant. Being with Hari Prasad Kanoria and hearing his story stirred something within me. I realized that to have a journey worth talking about, I needed to stop being tentative and come from the space he did. A space defined by faith in self and faith in God.

SREI taking off to global heights

Chapter 38

Faith in Self; Faith in God

Hari went to Vrindavan to get the blessings of Bihariji (Lord Krishna) and Ma Radha. He knew the proposal he had was good. So, there was an immaculate faith in self. At the same time, he had learnt ages ago that not a leaf stirred unless God willed it. Exuding confidence and humility he sought to move the mountains ahead of him in his journey as an entrepreneur.

When he came back to Delhi, he immediately met the official. All he had brought back from Vrindavan was one peda (an Indian sweetmeat) and a little chandan (sandalwood). He did not want the official to think that he was trying to bribe him. The officer readily accepted the peda and chandan but said, 'I am unable to give approval.'

As Hari came out, on the spur of the moment he decided to seek a meeting with the finance secretary and the finance minister. He had a lot of faith and knew things had to move. After waiting for an hour, he got an appointment and met them. Both of them knew Hari, but not very closely, as from the times when he was the president of the Calcutta Chamber of Commerce.

He explained the position to the finance secretary, stating clearly that just as the government wished to promote infrastructure, SREI wanted to contribute to that sector. He explained that he wanted to do it so that small and medium contractors too could be given a chance. If only bigger companies like L&T were given an opportunity, it would not do justice to the smaller organizations that wished to contribute to the infrastructure sector. Lastly, he said that SREI wanted to provide employment to many more people.

The finance secretary was convinced and asked him to meet the minister concerned. Hari met the minister who was convinced as well. He called the finance secretary to look into the matter. The finance secretary called the official and told him to give immediate approval to Hari's proposal.

A very happy Hari then went back to the official and said with humility, 'Please don't take my action of approaching the finance secretary and finance minister amiss. I know you have your limitations and also good intentions, hence I went to them.'

The official gave the order and that is how SREI came out with a public issue. The journey was far from over. In fact, it was just beginning.

But a 'sweet' beginning had been made. One that came with a single peda and some chandan, but brimming with the blessings of Lord Krishna and Ma Radha, and the determination of a man who epitomized faith in self and faith in God.

When I heard of this victory from Hari Prasad, something within me blossomed. I realized the power of thinking right. I also realized how important it is to communicate right. With a combination of the two so much can happen. I made a mental note to myself to use these in every situation of my life—be it personal or professional.

Chapter 39

Wedding Bells

Each child's wedding, for Hari, was of great importance. It was an opportunity to express his love to his children, as well as to the world at large. It was time to experience lavish spreads, deep love and immense bonding. He wanted every single wedding to be a memorable one and according to the family status, but not extravagant with pomp and show—and so it had been.

Hari did not have much of a financial standing then as the business was at a nascent stage and took much more out of them than it gave. However, the two flour mills helped in upholding the family's reputation. Hari's foresight to not resign from his position as the nominal head of the larger family business—with the name but no real power—helped immensely during this phase. He realized that having that kind of standing ensured that the children received proposals from families that were really held in respect in Kolkata.

The first wedding that took place in the Kanoria home was that of Hemant. Since he was a man of deep intelligence as well as emotional equipoise, Hari wanted Hemant to be married to a girl who would become his partner for life, holding his hand through all the ups and downs, just like Champa Devi had done for him.

Hemant had just crossed twenty-one. He was studying for his Bachelor's degree and also chartered accountancy. His paternal grandfather, Kedarnath, wanted Hemant to be married so that he could enjoy the presence of a granddaughter-in-law and, in course of time, a great-grandchild. There was a belief that one goes to Baikunth Dham (the celestial abode of Lord Vishnu and

Ma Laxmi) when they have experienced the joy of being with their great grandchild.

But Hemant was not willing. When a proposal came for him his eyes got moist. He could not say a word. Hari could feel his deep concern regarding his studies and business. To rescue him from that situation, his younger brother Sanjeev quietly took on several responsibilities to enter the *grishastha ashram*. Champa Devi was a bit concerned as to how the marriage would be accomplished in the midst of their financial crisis. However, having faith in Hari and God she reconciled herself to do the best for her eldest son with her personal savings.

On 22 April 1984, Hemant was married to the beautiful and charming Madhulika. Her demeanour spoke of a quiet grace and strength which appealed to Hari, and the moment he saw her, he knew she would be the eldest daughter-in-law of the family. One who would set the benchmark for others.

The next in line was Sanjeev the adventurous, Sanjeev the rebel. He wanted to go to London for further medical studies. Hari, as always, was reluctant to send his dear son to a place where they knew no one. To hold him back Hari said, 'It is time for your marriage.'

To this Sanjeev replied, 'I am going to London in twenty days. I will get married if you can find me a girl in twenty days. Else, I will leave unmarried. Either way, I am going.' After his father Kedarnath's demise in 1986, Hari felt a sense of loneliness towards performing his children's marriage, however, he determined to do his best.

Sanjeev was raising the stakes, but it was his father who was at the other end. A worthy opponent. Hari decided, no matter what, he would find a bride for his wife within that period. If he had to go to London, at least he would go with his life partner and not go alone. He told Sanjeev, 'As of now I have no clue how I will do it, but I have faith in God and I will get you married in twenty days.'

Sanjeev smirked.

There was a renowned advocate who was a friend of Kedarnath too. Hari would visit him often for tax related talks. He recommended a beautiful girl from a good family who would be a perfect match for Sanjeev. Hari got excited—and immediately agreed for a meeting. At that time Sanjeev was staying at the Hastings office to study and did not come home at all. His meals were being sent there.

One afternoon Sanjeev was sitting draped in a towel, happily sipping a cup of tea when unexpectedly the parents of the girl showed up. They wanted to see who Sanjeev was, and when the office boy pointed him out they were amused to find their potential son-in-law in a state of undress. Even then they found him to be handsome and appealing. They invited Hari's family to see their daughter.

Hari cajoled Sanjeev and also put Hemant on the job of convincing him to meet the girl. Hemant, Sanjeev and a few others from the Kanoria family went to see the girl. Sanjeev got angry, saying, 'You are showing me a girl who is like Trijata (a demoness in the Ramayana).' Sanjeev did not mean any disrespect to the girl, he was simply expressing his annoyance at his father. Hari was regretting having arranged the meeting on the word of a known person. He was at a loss to know how to find his demanding, eccentric son a wife. The clock was ticking but he had full faith in Ma Kali.

Finally, when only a few days remained, a friend of Hari suggested a girl from Indonesia. He said the girl was wonderfully well brought up and beautiful, but the family did not have a status matching the Kanorias. They were simple, humble people hailing from the holy city of Varanasi. Hari said, it doesn't matter; let the boy and girl meet, and if they like each other, we are willing to go ahead.

Everything was arranged in haste, with Hari rushing from Delhi to Kolkata to make the meeting happen. Sanjeev met Sangita for the first time and they spoke for an hour.

Hari was eagerly awaiting Sanjeev's response after the meeting.

He saw Sanjeev looking angry and his heart sank. Once again, he was sure, Sanjeev would say no. However, much to Hari's surprise and delight, Sanjeev said, 'I am so angry Father! You have made me meet such a good girl. I had thought that you would not be able to find a girl of my choice and I would go to London as a bachelor. But now that you have managed even this impossible feat, I will marry her and then both of us will go to London. Please arrange the marriage within fifteen days.'

Fifteen days for a wedding! That too, a Kanoria wedding.

Hari, as always, was up to the challenge. The girl's parents were shell-shocked. They said, 'We live in Indonesia, how will we arrange the wedding in such a short period?' Since Sangita had liked Sanjeev, they wanted things to work out, but a wedding in two weeks? Was it possible? Hari told them not to worry and that he would manage everything. 'You just come with your family and friends,' he said.

And that is how Sanjeev Kanoria, within a month of deciding to get married, actually got married and left for London with his beautiful bride, much to the entire family's joy.

The three weddings that followed had their own share of love, laughter and excitement: Sunil got married to the soft-spoken but strong-willed Sunita, Sujit found his soulmate in the beautiful and enterprising Divita, and Manisha tied the knot with Parashar who she believes is her soulmate in many ways.

Hemant and Madhulika

Sanjeev and Sangita

WEDDING BELLS • 97

Sunil and Sunita

Sujit and Divita

Parashar and Manisha

Chapter 40

Return on Investment

There is a saying, 'If children are an investment, grandchildren and great-grandchildren are the returns on one's investment, dearer than the investment itself.'

In many ways, so it was for Hari. When the Kanoria home heard the first little cry of the next generation (Siddhishree, born to Hemant and Madhulika on 30 April 1985), both Hari and Champa were beside themselves with joy. There seemed to be an invisible music playing through the walls of the Kanoria home, and dancers who couldn't be seen celebrating all around. Hari felt his heart swell with love as he held the little baby in his hands.

He had the opportunity to experience this happiness many times in his life. The third generation of Kanorias in Hari's family consists of nine youngsters, each so unique and yet so connected with the culture of the family that anyone who sees them is left feeling awestruck. Hemant and Madhulika are the proud parents of Siddhi and Raghav. Mukund and Vatsal are the children of Sanjeev and Sangita. Anant and Avani are the children of Sunil and Sunita, and Sujit and Divita have a boy and a girl—Nitya and Yagyesh. Manisha and Parashar are the parents of young Vedant. The fourth generation made its entry when Rajveka was born to Siddhi on 18 September 2012.

The growing-up years of all these tots was filled with memories of the Kanoria grandeur, the learning that their parents and grandparents imparted to them in all the ways they could, the feeling of oneness, love, laughter and numerous family holidays and festivals. Each grandchild has at least a dozen stories to share about Dadu (paternal grandfather) or Nanu (maternal grandfather, in the case of Vedant) and they have seen Hari play multiple roles in their life—from their friend to their teacher; from their confidant to their mentor; from their partner in innumerable 'mastis' of life to their inspiration. Each grandchild believes that Dadu, or Nanu, is one of his or her greatest blessings in life.

What sheer delight it is to see Hari Prasad Kanaria relating with his grandchildren. Age seems to crumble like cookies between them, the generation gap is non-existent. Together they flow, like a spring, gurgling happily all the way.

I observed something beautiful. Whenever Hari Prasad Kanaria spoke of his grandchildren, his countenance would begin to beam with love and pride.

When he speaks about his life or achievements, it's so matter of fact, like telling the truth. However, the moment it is about the children, and especially the nine grandchildren and one great grandchild, it's like the clouds have parted to let the brilliant sunshine in. It is most beautiful—and heartening.

Grandchildren

Hari and the family—strong ties that bind

Sowing the seeds of spirituality: Hari with grandchildren

Hari with Raghav

With Anant in Boston

Hari with Nitya, Avani and Mukund

Chapter 41

Vishnu Loka

It is believed in the Hindu traditions that when a man lives his life in a pious and correct way, the end is always peaceful.

We could take this a step forward with the Kanorias. As mentioned earlier, when Hari's grandfather died, the last words on his lips were 'Hari! Hari!' Whether he was calling out to Hari, his grandson, or his Lord, no one will ever know, and yet, to know that his last words were so beautiful goes to show the life he had led. According to the Vedas, when one calls out the name of Hari or Narayan or any other name of Lord Vishnu at the time of death, one goes to Vishnu Loka (Vishnu's abode) in their afterlife.

For Hari's father too the end was nothing short of mystical.

Hari's family is originally from a village called Khurana Kanore. There are about 250 steps that lead one to the top of the hill where there is a beautiful temple of Ma Durga, who is also the Kul Devi (family deity) of the Kanorias. As mentioned earlier, the village is at a distance of about twenty km from Mahendragarh, now in Haryana.

It was a practice in the family, rather in the community, to visit the temple of Ma Durga in Khurana Kanore after the birth of a child and before marriage.

All his life Hari's father had been a devotee of Durga Ma. From the pujos in Kolkata to the innermost chambers of his heart, she existed everywhere, and he believed that it was her blessings that had made possible the life they led: One so full of love, laughter and abundance of every form and kind.

In the year 1986, he visited the temple with one of his sons who urged him to not climb the 250 steps. However, Kedarnath seemed to have some kind of a gleam in his eyes. There was a strange feeling of knowing in him, an inexplicable calm. He huffed and puffed, stretching himself beyond his physical means and finally made it to the top.

However, as soon as he reached the sanctum sanctorum, before his beloved Durga Ma, he collapsed. Although many people tried to help and call for a doctor, it was clear that he had found his creator, the child had found his mother, and, in her bosom, he had let go of life. Kedarnath was only sixty-six years of age.

The entire journey—of being a son, a father, a husband, a brother, a friend, a notable entrepreneur—came to an end as Kedarnath's ashes mingled with earth in a final act of surrender and devotion.

The 250 steps were almost like his final pilgrimage—and the pilgrim did justice to it.

Hari Prasad's eyes were moist as he reminisced about it. I could feel the love, the pride, the loss and the longing in him in those moments. Even at 80, there was a little child in him missing father. I knew he was with me physically but mentally he was there—at the hilltop abode of Ma Durga, watching his father, as he bade them a final goodbye. Like his departed father, Hari Prasad's love for Ma Durga also knows no bounds.

Hari's father

Kuldevi Maa Durga, Khurana (Mahendragarh)

Chapter 42

Taking Wings

In the year 1992, along with his friend, P. M. Singhvi, Hari went to London and New York to market the public issue. Sanjeev was there working as a doctor. P.M. Singhvi's elder brother, L.M. Singhvi, the Indian high commissioner in the UK (1992-1993) also happened to be in London. Hemant too accompanied Hari. They were of the view that people abroad had the capacity to invest. Moreover, foreign investment would create a good brand for the company in India too. Hari's company ended up raising Rs 2 crore from the public issue.

At that time, both Hemant and Sunil were deeply involved in the company's affairs. Father and sons were working out of office in Hastings and Burrabazar where the larger family was. Then their personal medium-sized office shifted to another place in central Kolkata. In a room having four tables, father and sons used to sit. The name of their company was given around this time: SREI is the abbreviation for Sri Radha Krishna Export Industries (SREI). It was Hemant's idea.

In fact, as mentioned earlier, from the time Hemant was an 18-year-old college student, he had been like Hari's right-hand man. He was intelligent and patient, someone Hari could rely on to shoulder all the responsibilities, just as his father had relied on him. At the age of nineteen, while Sunil was completing his graduation and studying chartered accountancy, he had started helping his father.

The growth of infrastructure was slow but steady. The entrepreneur in Hari knew that it was a time to be patient and take measured steps. Hari and Hemant regularly met bankers, senior officials and anyone who they thought could help to get things moving. They would be asked to wait outside by their secretaries, sometimes for months, and still nothing would move. However, they did not lose hope. They continued to knock at all the doors possible, knowing that sooner or later they would make progress.

And they did. Their hard work, patience and faith paid off. In just a few years people began to know them and appointments and assignments were easier to come by. In time, SREI also got into the business of financing of infrastructure—heavy equipment like cranes, bulldozers, road-making machines and the like. They were among the first few companies to foray into this sector. The word 'SREI' stands for 'shrestha', the very best, and also 'shrey', to give credit.

Projects for financing infrastructure held appeal for bankers, bureaucrats and politicians. They were for inclusive and sustainable growth of infrastructure, and for solving the problems of financing for medium and small contractors and enterprises.

What began as a small office with four tables and maybe two or three staff members soon grew into a much bigger organization. Initially all the work was handled by the trio, but gradually they started hiring, and that is how SREI began to spread its wings.

As an entrepreneur myself, I listened to all these stories with a keen interest. It was very fascinating for me to know what goes into the making of a prominent company—how the foundation is laid, what kind of thoughts and emotions are invested, and what courage. What we usually see is the final product, and here I was getting the chance to share this knowledge with all of you. It was amazing. And yes, very inspiring. I made a mental note of all that I wanted to do once I got back.

A landmark date for SREI

SREI listing at the London Stock Exchange

Chapter 43

What More, What Next?

One of the most important characteristics of an entrepreneur's mindset is to keep asking oneself, 'What more, what next?' And Hari was a master at this. From the smallest of projects to the bigger ones, he saw each one as a God-send and did not refuse anything.

In 1997, Hari thought *Why limit SREI to the domestic markets—why not try for foreign institutional investment*? The World Bank has its private sector arm namely, the International Finance Corporation (IFC). They invest and give money to developing countries. Hari and Hemant found out that IFC had been giving funds to projects in Russia and India.

Hari sensed that there could be scope for big growth there so he went to Washington DC and met the officers there. One of them happened to be from West Bengal and the other was from Delhi. Unfortunately, their response was similar to what Hari had once faced with the government official in Delhi. They told him, 'Sorry, Mr Kanoria, your business is too small. Nothing can be done.'

Hari being Hari, he never took no for an answer. And so he tried to convince them by giving them numerous examples. However, they were not willing to budge from their stand. Hari then requested for a meeting with the CEO of the IFC, Jannik Lindbaek.

Most people would not have the courage to ask for an appointment, without any prior intimation, with someone of that stature. Hari's thinking was, if someone else has to reject my idea or proposal, it is okay, but why should I deny it to myself?

The secretary of the CEO requested Hari to wait for an hour, saying he would try his best to arrange a meeting. He returned to inform Hari that the CEO would see him. The CEO was a man of depth and genuine intent. Hari explained everything about India—the market, the infrastructure situation, and the opportunities. If there was one thing Hari always took great pride in, it was his in-depth knowledge. His research was thorough and he knew that what he was presenting was viable and made great sense. Yes, the company was small, but the future held immense possibilities.

The CEO approved a sanction for SREI and that was SREI's first project funding from a foreign institution. It brought a lot of credibility to SREI, even though the amount was not very significant. It was a big turning point in the lives of the Kanorias, as a family and as a business. The world had just opened up to them.

Somehow the thought process of not rejecting the self really appealed to me. I could think of so many situations in my life where before the world could say no to me, in my own mind I had said no to myself.

When he shared this chapter of his life, it actually put me in a pensive mood; it made me recall a quote I had read of Warren Buffet which basically said that there weren't just two columns in life—one which said 'Projects won' and the second that said 'Projects lost'. Rather, there was a third column also, titled 'Opportunities missed'. We don't realize that so many of our ideas or thoughts could have been the next big thing, but they never materialized because we rejected them ourselves before the world rejected us.

I realized it takes great courage and a tremendous amount of self-belief to go all out to make a dream or vision come true—and the first step is to never give up on yourself. Like Will Smith tells his son in *The Pursuit of Happyness*, 'You got a dream, you got to protect it. People can't do something themselves, they'll say: "You can't do it." You want something, go get it.'

Chapter 44

The Power of Pen

As mentioned before, Hari had developed a love for writing from a very young age. When he was the President of the Calcutta Chamber of Commerce and an office bearer in many other organizations, he had written several speeches about the problems of the nation, industry, business, and the social and political spheres. He craved his own magazine so that he could express his views on various matters to decision-makers across the country.

In February 1995, he launched a weekly, *Business Economics*, in a tabloid format, with sixteen pages which soon grew to twenty-four pages on popular demand. In February 2008, the tabloid became a fortnightly magazine reflecting global aspirations. *Business Economics* is globally circulated and Hari is the editor-in-chief.

When he was the president of the Akhil Bharatiya Marwari Sammelan, he used to write on various subjects for publication in their magazine, *Samaj Vikas*. He has also written a couple of plays on the subject of women and family life, depicting how culture and spirituality make life happy for the entire family. The two plays were: *Our Beloved Daughters-in-Law* and *Our Beloved Daughters*. Both plays were enacted and were widely acclaimed in Kolkata.

One of the most incredible feelings for me as the author of this book was to observe how all the dots connected. When he was barely in his teens, Hari's father encouraged him to start writing a personal diary. His education in both Presidency College as well as Xavier's improved his English skills, and he had always had a liking for reading from a young age. All of this culminated in him becoming the editor-in-chief of a popular magazine. My guru, Mahatria, always says, at every stage, life is preparing us for something; what it is, remains for us to unravel.

As Hari Prasad Kanoria reminisced about his life, we could see a sparkle in his eyes as a seemingly insignificant incident from the past has come together to give immense meaning to his life as it is today.

Hari Prasad Kanoria, the then President of All India Marwari Federation

The cover of Business Economics magazine

Chapter 45

Of Failures and Learnings

One of the integral aspects of a successful business is failure. Paradoxical as it may sound, this is the truth. Unless a business undergoes several ups and downs, touches peaks and valleys, it can never become a notable one. And so it was with Hari.

He recalls an instance when his company was giving loans to businessmen. A person came to meet them while Hari was with his sons. He wanted a credit of Rs 20 lakh, which they sanctioned. However, after four or five days he returned, asking for more.

This time Hari questioned him, 'What are you manufacturing?' He asked the question in the presence of his sons so that they too could learn from the experience. The man replied, 'I am manufacturing small televisions.'

To this Hari responded, 'How have you produced televisions against a loan of only Rs 20 lakh? How many units have you produced and what is the selling price of each? Moreover, how did you manage to produce so many units in such a short time?'

The man sat there, flabbergasted and unsure. Hari immediately grasped that it was a bogus idea and there was no foundation to the business at all. Unfortunately, a person on Hari's staff had already introduced him to the bank as someone whose initial loan Hari had approved. That had led to the bank sanctioning a second loan to him directly without the knowledge of Hari.

Predictably, he could not repay the loan. The bank lost money and Hari's reputation was affected, even though Hari had not been involved in any direct transactions of the bank. Also, he had not introduced the party to the bank.

Someone lesser might have felt low, but not Hari. In fact, he categorically says that business never makes him go through the vagaries of emotions. He sees business as just that—business. He does not allow it to become his be all and end all. Otherwise, with so many businesses and so many fluctuations, he would constantly be at his wits' end.

By its very nature, business comes with uncertainty. No matter what, one can never know what will work, what won't work, or even how long something will work. Several of Hari's flour mills, among the largest in India, had been closed down. They were nurtured by the toil of his youth. His father used to say that their flour mills would remain their safety net for seven generations. All of them closed down in the time of the second generation itself due to the politics of trade unions and state governments.

Some businesses flourished beyond belief, some disappointed beyond imagination. What was, was.

'I see business, as business,' says Hari Prasad. And in that sentence, I think, he says it all.

Chapter 46
Turning Information into Opportunity

Like his father, every morning Hari read close to five newspapers in languages ranging from English, Hindi and Bengali.

Hari had learnt Bengali from his father's steno-typist in 1960-1961 when he was a college student. He would come to office after college hours to learn the art and science of running a business. He had grown fond of Shyama Sangeet, a genre of devotional songs in Bengal dedicated to the Ma Kali, the songs of the saint-poet Ramaprasad, and the Baul songs of the mystic, Lalon Fakir. To that end, he was eager to learn the language. He picked up the language without any difficulty, even though he had done the major part of his schooling in Bihar.

He had this firm belief that information was knowledge and knowledge was power. He also had a knack for converting information into opportunity. In 1995, when Hari was going through the newspapers with his usual vigour, he saw an item that the government had decided to appoint independent directors in banks. Hari wanted to try out that role as he felt it would give him a great deal of exposure to a new world and a chance to execute his role responsibly in uncharted territory.

At that time there were some Union ministers and bureaucrats who were known to Hari. He requested them to recommend his name—and they readily did so. There was a vetting process in place and Hari had to furnish many documents, including his income tax filings. Fortunately for Hari, all his documents were fine and he was appointed as a director in the United Bank of India for a period of six years.

He resigned from SREI for that period to avoid any conflict of interest as it was a finance company. He often remarked that it was a very enriching experience for him.

Everything began with one single report in the newspaper, and that was why Hari would always emphasize the importance of being good information gatherers. Only when one knows what is going on can one—convert information into opportunity like an alchemist.

I have had the pleasure of staying in the Kanoria home on several occasions. It delighted me to see how Hari Prasad would read the newspapers during breakfast with family members and initiate interesting discussions around the news.

His newspaper-reading style is rather funny. As he scans the paper, he expertly filters out the irrelevant from the relevant. He reads the newspaper like he is reading an important financial report—nodding, correcting, highlighting and signing on a piece that has been read carefully. He is nothing if not an eccentric human and it is fun to watch him do this ritual in the mornings.

Chapter 47

Are You Ready for the Risk?

One attitude that probably differentiates an entrepreneur from someone in service is their appetite for risks. Hari believed that risk-taking is an integral, almost day-to-day part of business. Unless one has the ability to take up this challenge, one should not call oneself a businessman.

Hari had not studied business management from any premier or popular management institute. He was extremely proud of his alma maters and the teachers from whom he had learnt the ropes of work.

His teachers were his grandfather and father.

His grandfather's words remain etched in his mind, 'Take care of the overheads—salary, rent and interest. These eat into a businessman's resources. There would be a boom followed by recession every three years, and this cycle would continue, with some years being much more turbulent than others.'

His father's advice also stayed with him: 'Learn the ABC of it—'A' means accounts, 'B' means business and 'C' means co-operation'.

Hari respected and believed both of them. He observed them closely and absorbed their wisdom. He understood that business was not about learning from books but about learning in the field. These two men with great business acumen taught him a lot.

Risk-taking is a talent one develops when one observes others closely, watch deals being closed and executed, and are a part of different conversations pertaining to work. It helps one understand what is going on in the minds of others, develop a vision for the future and evaluate the pros and cons effectively.

For instance, SREI entered car financing in a very limited way—however they did not go ahead with it in some areas of Uttar Pradesh and Bihar despite having good contacts. The reason for this was that in these areas there were mafias that would have a car financed and then sell the car and its parts and vanish with the money. The lesson being that has to be aware of one's surroundings to take the right decisions.

Hari firmly believed that one of the most important aspects of decision-making was thorough homework. While he allowed intuition to guide him, it was always intensive hard work that he relied on. In fact, he recalled a conversation with a close friend who once remarked, you have always had luck on your side as far as business is concerned. To this Hari replied thoughtfully, the results you see show just one per cent of the truth. What you don't see is the ninety-nine per cent hard work that has gone into making this dream come true. He added with a laugh, 'I am lucky because I am hard-working and blessed by Ma Kali!'

Hari believed that there was no such thing as lack of opportunity. He would say, if you work hard enough, opportunities will come knocking at your door. All that matters is absolute hard work, along with faith in self and God.

We often hear people say, work hard and everything will fall into place. However, I had seen enough people work hard and still not reach where they are capable of reaching. I realized there are several nuances to one becoming what they can—and being a risk-taker after doing enough homework is another important aspect. Having belief in oneself and God—is yet another. When all these fall in place, miraculous growth becomes possible.

Chapter 48

The Way Forward

Every business has its own unique trajectory. There are turning points and life defining moments which significantly impact the journey of every business.

What were these for SREI?

Hari had a single sentence answer: 'Every moment was a turning point for SREI.'

He followed a simple formula which took SREI from its original four-table office space to the position of a large listed company. His formula was as follows:

Step 1: Gather information
Step 2: Find opportunities
Step 3: Do your research and evaluate the business model
Step 4: Work hard
Step 5: Have faith in self, and in God
Step 6: Succeed.

Hari shared stories about how each time they would get some kind of information about a possible growth opportunity, they would jump at it to see if it made sense for them. There was no question of laziness, doubt or procrastination. In business, the quicker you make a move, the faster everything happens.

Hari and his sons always believed in being the forerunners in every field they explored. If things looked promising, they didn't waste time over-analysing it. Rather, they went in with complete faith. After receiving some funding from the IFC in 1997, they didn't stop there. Smelling an opportunity, the same year they also went to various other countries with their proposal and received strategic equity investments from the German government's Development Finance Company (DEG), and the Netherlands government's Development Finance Company (FMO), among others.

What set them apart at every stage was their in-depth research based on hard facts and their promise to work hard towards the goal just as it was shown on the blue-print. Gradually, banks started getting interested in SREI and were open to financing them. One became two, two became many. In the same way, vendors too became interested. SREI began to earn the trust and respect of all its partners.

However, through it all—Hari and his sons never allowed themselves to become foolhardy or impulsive. Being cautious and evaluating their risks remained an integral part of their work ethic even through the tremendous highs when it is easy to go with the flow and even lose oneself. Success and money can be quite intoxicating, but Hari was immune to both; he saw all the abundance as a grace and blessing and did not allow it to go to his head. He had learnt the value of simplicity amidst abundance from none other than his grandfather and father, and he lives it each day of his life.

Hari and his sons Hemant, Sanjeev, Sunil and Sujit

Chapter 49

The Strength of a Grass

In 2008, there was a global financial crisis. Every company, in every industry was hit. Many of them crumbled and collapsed. However, SREI stood strong through everything.

Hari compared himself and his people to grass. When the worst of storms come, the trees are hit. Even the ones with the strongest of roots are uprooted. At such times, like grass, one needs to lie low.

SREI withstood the turbulence with the help of Hari's mantra in life—faith in the self, faith in hard work, and faith in God.

Many SREI executives and top-level management were perturbed with all that was happening in the country and the world. However, both Hari and Hemant remained calm. They knew something that everyone in business should know—bad times are as real as good times, and they are short-lived. Once you show staying power, the storm leaves you alone, realizing that you cannot be touched. Much like the humble grass—so closely connected to earth that there is no scope of it being harmed by the storm.

Hari was well versed in facing challenges right from a young age. He had seen his grandfather deal with numerous issues, and then his father too. He had nerves of steel and knew that challenges were part and parcel of doing business. After all, entrepreneurship was not for the weak-hearted; it was for those who could withstand the vagaries of life and business.

He often quoted from the Mahabharata when things were not so favourable. He would say, 'Even when God is on your side, you have to do what you have to do. Life was never easy for the Pandavas, even with Lord Krishna by their side. They had to face all kinds of adversities and suffer innumerable hardships before victory was theirs. When Gods and Goddesses didn't have it easy, why should we as mere mortals?'

He also re-iterated that life, by its very design, was not meant to be a bed of roses. How ordinary and boring would a life like that be? Instead, life was meant to be rollercoaster, sometimes going so high that you feel your face is being touched by the clouds, and sometimes so low that you don't know if tomorrow will. And yet tomorrow does come. It has to.

SREI stood strong, no matter what. All those people who had predicted its collapse, wonder what happened?

The grass always survives to tell the story of the storm.

I have often seen in my own life that when I did not give in to a problem and had faith in life's plans for me, eventually, the problem gave in to me. Staying power is important not just for business but for every aspect of life—be it health, wealth, relationships, or spirituality.

Chapter 50

Surviving the Storm

SREI, over the last decade, has grown in every dimension possible. Whichever city you may be in, it is likely that you will see the SREI logo, in bright red, on some hoarding or building, or supporting an event connected with some social cause or the other.

There is a wonderful concept that, Mahatria, a spiritual guru of international repute has come up with. It is called the 'imaginary finishing line'. He says life has its own way of testing and segregating the winners from the also-rans. It draws a finishing line as if to say, 'Hey, runner, you have reached the end!' The mediocre or average ones, who do not have much self-confidence or courage, believe this to be true, and they stop. However, the legends—the men and women of great conviction—know that this is not an end but simply a bend, and they persist. They cross the finishing line knowing it is but an imaginary finishing line, and in doing so, something within them undergoes a breakthrough. They redefine the grammar of life. They create miracles, and become the names we hear of. They become an inspiration to the rest of the world.

This is what happened with Hari Prasad Kanoria and his sons, too. They did not wilt under pressure. They did not cave in to the storm of challenges, and challenges came from everywhere. They just persisted and kept going.

There were journeys the Kanorias embarked upon that an average person would have possibly abandoned; there were tidal waves they rose above which any ordinary person would have drowned under. Holding on to their faith in self, in associates, in hard work, and God, they went on.

The result? Today, SREI is a beacon of hope for businesses across the world. As a holistic and integrated infrastructure institution, SREI offers all possible services in the infrastructure value chain, medium and small enterprises, under one umbrella. In fact, SREI is the only organization to be present across all the touch points of the infrastructure canvas.

From financing projects to rentals, from advisory services to creating innovative programmes for customers, SREI is at the forefront of the infrastructure sector. Their aim is to provide holistic solutions that are essential for creating a future filled with the possibilities of a brighter tomorrow.

And to think it all began with one man wondering what to do with himself and his life when his family was not willing to support him.

What I find most incredible about Hari Prasad's journey is his spirit. Usually when you see a face, it tells the story of the pain it has endured—the cracks of faith, the grief and the hurt show up along with all the beauty. But negativity brought upon by the behaviour of the larger family seemed to have left no scar on him. He seemed to be swathed and protected by some invisible grace which has carried his spirit—so vibrant, so child-like and so untouched—from one end of the spectrum to the other. Like a lotus blooming in all its glory, even amidst filth.

Chapter 51

When Life Hands You Lemons...

In the case of Hari, the proverbial phrase, when life gives you lemons, make lemonade, is absolutely true, be it in business or in family life, at home or on a holiday. In fact, he would it a step forward and would also make some lemon 'chaat' to go with the lemonade!

One of the most wonderful aspects of his personality, to me, was his child-like exuberance. He doesn't make work look like work—it comes alive with fun, humour and eccentricity in his presence.

Many years ago in 1975, he visited Puri the coastal city in Odisha with his teenage children and his brother-in-law. It is a city which has tremendous religious and spiritual significance and millions throng there from across the globe to experience the various festivities and rituals that surround Jagannath Temple.

Like all other seekers, Hari and his brother-in-law too proceeded for a dip in the ocean. However, unlike everyone else, Hari refused to hold hands in a human chain as the sea was exceptionally rough that day. He fell and broke his leg.

Anyone else in his situation would have been utterly frustrated to have their leg in a cast and hobble around with a stick on a vacation, but not our dear Hari. Instead, he decided to make the most of his limited movement. Wearing saffron clothes and many beaded necklaces, he sat at the shore with many boxes of sweets.

As expected, people mistook the balding, happy-looking charismatic man for a sage and bowed before him for his blessings. He, in turn, played his role well, blessing each head with a thwack from his stick and handing out sweetmeats. He had a good laugh about the entire experience.

What could have seemed like an unnecessary malady—became cause for mirth because, for Hari, every moment in life is for celebration.

In fact, because Hari kept looking for reasons to be happy, life kept presenting him with several opportunities for the same.

Hari's heart was filled with joy when the marriage proposal for his eldest grandchild—Siddhishree—daughter of his eldest son Hemant arrived from Shri Bishwanath Jhunjhunwala, father of Archit Jhunjhunwala. The family Purohit had also suggested this alliance.

Hari and Hemant happened to meet Archit at a marriage function and found him to be very smart, intelligent as well as highly educated. The families, as well as the bride and groom in question, got along beautifully and the marriage was held on 12 July 2008.

Siddhishree's brother Raghav, too, was approaching a marriageable age and Hari wanted him to find the right girl. On Raghav's birthday celebration, Hari interacted with all his young friends and found one girl called Shruti to be very intelligent, simple and impressive. He somehow had the thought, 'This girl would complement Raghav well!,' but did not voice it.

Turns out, he didn't have to. After about two months Raghav approached his parents in Switzerland with a lot of hesitation and nervousness and shared that he was in love with a girl and wished for them to take the proposal to her parents, as her father was looking for a right match for her. Hemant told Raghav that he would only be able to take a decision after discussing with Hari.

The moment Hari heard the name 'Shruti' he was thrilled. He couldn't believe how right his thoughts and instincts were. As per the Hindu religion a grandson's marriage brings happiness and a grand-daughter-in-law is an embodiment of Goddess Lakshmi. Hari could not stop beaming and rejoicing on that wonderful

128 • HAPPINESS IN THE AGE OF AMBITION

day—29 January 2015—when Raghav and Shruti tied the knot with the love and blessings of both the families.

As I listened to him, seeing the animated way in which he recounted the tale, I couldn't help but burst out laughing. I had experienced this side to him umpteen times. Stuck in traffic? He would make the most of it by reading books or taking that quick power nap. Caught off guard by a situation? He would immediately try to see how much fun or learning could be derived from it. I think this is the thought process that makes legends. There is never a dull moment around them. Literally.

Hari with Champa Devi

Archit and Siddhi

Raghav and Shruti

Chapter 52

Adventures and Misadventures

Nobody's life is exempt from unfavourable circumstances. Every life has its share of peaks and valleys, and the true mark of a wonderful explorer is one who takes adventures and misadventures in his stride.

Once when Hari was in Paris, he had a terrible experience with a cab driver. The drivers there are known to often cheat unsuspecting travellers and it was just Hari's luck to have found himself in the company of one such cab driver.

The hotel reception had mentioned the amount Hari would have to pay for taking a cab from the hotel to the airport. Hari kept that amount in his wallet and set off. However, the driver took him from a different, much longer route and demanded a fare which was almost double the amount he had been expecting.

Hari didn't have enough Euros and the cabbie refused to accept US dollars. He had to take a detour to withdraw the money from an ATM. All of this led to an unexpected delay and he missed his flight to Zurich—he was to meet some clients there. Since he did not arrive in Zurich, his clients—got so worried that they actually sent a message to Hari's family that Mr Hari may have been abducted!

The beauty of being 'abducted Hari' was that he didn't let situations like these get the better of him. Rather, in a calm way he would think through and see how best to get out of a bad situation. This gave him the clarity to deal with the matter at hand in a mature way. Within a few hours he was able to reach Zurich and let everyone know that nothing that drastic had happened to him. Yet.

One thing was sure: wherever Hari went, action happened. Life was never dull or boring for Hari—or for the people around him. There was always, I repeat, always, something happening.

Hari in Paris with the disciples of ISKCON

Chapter 53

Food for Soul

Swami Vivekananda has had a very profound impact on the life of Hari Prasad Kanoria. His philosophy, his quotes and his poetry have made a home for themselves in his heart and soul, and he believes in living by them as far as possible.

Two of Hari's grandsons, Anant and Raghav, got admission in Boston University. The family had taken an apartment there so that they could pursue their studies and family members could stay with them during their visits. Boston as a city had fascinated Hari for years. It was where Swami Vivekananda had stayed because it was cheaper compared to cities like Chicago and New York.

Hari felt at home in Boston and, in a strange way, he felt connected to his source of faith there. The city further strengthened his love for and faith in Swamiji, who, almost a century ago, had walked the same stone pathways and breathed the same pristine air.

Right next to the Boston University was the Vedanta Institute and Hari loved going there to just sit around and read books. Since he didn't have much to do there—his only means of making his days fulfilling was to read all the books he had brought from India, and then buy some more.

Along with exploring his spiritual depth in Boston, Hari also developed his culinary skills. He did not enjoy eating at restaurants every day—and he did not want his grandsons to eat so much of outside food either. There was only one solution—he had to don a chef's hat.

He made pasta, spaghetti, roti, vegetables. In fact, on the day of Pitra Paksh (a day when food is made in remembrance of one's ancestors), Hari, who had never experimented with cooking before, actually made kheer and poorie (elaborate Indian dishes). He also went to a temple thirty km away from Boston to mark the day.

Boston was good for Hari, exceedingly good. It gave him enough food for the soul—and gave him an opportunity to cook, both of which made him feel great about himself.

Father, grandfather, great grandfather, lawyer, businessman, author, and chef—Hari Prasad is one of those people who seem to wear many hats so beautifully.

Chef Hari—What's Cooking

Chapter 54

A Help in Time...

After Anant completed his course at Boston University, he came back to India. He was there for close to four years and Hari joined him on several occasions. He fell in love with the city and wanted to be there as much as possible. We all have that one city where everything feels like home to us, and it seems to bring out the best in us. For Hari, it was Boston for sure.

Manisha visited him once along with Vedant. One evening as they were walking to a grocery store, Hari noticed an old woman struggling with two big shopping bags. She was frail and the bags looked heavy. Immediately Hari told Vedant, 'Go Beta, help the lady. Carry the bags for her!'

Vedant did as he was told and the lady looked most grateful. Hari and Manisha were watching the entire scene from the sidelines. As Vedant helped her put the bags in her car, the lady gave him five dollars. Young Vedant didn't really know what to do, but before he could take a decision, he heard a loud voice (belonging to his grandfather) say, 'Dear Lady! Please give this money to the church! We don't need it. I am a billionaire myself. My grandson just wanted to help you.'

The lady looked a little startled. She had meant well. Hari realized that, softened immediately and said, 'Please excuse my tone. All I want to say is we have no need for this money. Please give it to someone who will use it better. Give it as charity!' The lady smiled and said she would do so.

Vedant didn't know what exactly had transpired, but he knew one thing: Even a simple walk with his grandfather had to be one filled with fun, drama and learning.

With Vedant in Boston

Hari with Vedant in Boston

Chapter 55

Lessons in Divinity

One day as Hari was walking around Boston, like he usually did during his visits, he was stunned and amazed to find the Boston University School of Theology. Curious and excited, he walked in and requested a meeting with the director

He was so happy to see that the director was extremely rooted, calm and patient. She explained in detail about all the scriptures and courses that were taught there and how they helped people from across the globe find a home in spirituality—and deepen their understanding of love, compassion and service.

Hari was amazed. He had only dreamt of such a place, and he couldn't believe it actually existed. She then said, 'Mr Hari, I will make you meet someone very interesting!'

She called a youngster to her office. He hailed from South Africa and was pursuing a degree in Divinity. As he conversed with Hari, Hari felt two deep emotions at the same time: The first was awe at the way the youngster was able to articulate all his thoughts and the depth of his understand was beautiful.

The second emotion was shame. Hari felt that India was a country which was the very source of spirituality and yet it was so far away from creating such splendid organizations. He felt as an Indian that too much time had been wasted over petty emotions and discrimination and hence India was unable to rise to its truest strength and potential—of being a spiritual superpower. India was the original land of spiritual wisdom and yet it had failed to teach its citizens the value of and love for all religions which would end all wars, without and within.

The next few days were ones of sheer bliss and peace for

Hari. He went there daily, studied with the students, interacted with the faculty, sometimes sharing and at other times absorbing, and kept growing his love for his favourite subject: spirituality.

He remembers those days with a happy smile and admits, 'I never felt alone while I was there—even though Champa wasn't there and my grandson was busy. The days were filled with God—and it completed me in ways I cannot even imagine!'

So enriching was his time there that it energized Hari to write the book titled *Enlightenment—A Journey Within Through Service*. It was released by the former president of India, Dr A.P.J. Abdul Kalam during the Fourth World Confluence of Humanity, Power and Spirituality, held in Kolkata in 2012, organized by the Kanoria Foundation. Over one hundred thousand copies of the book have been published and distributed since then, and many people have found answers to their spiritual quest through this book.

Inspired by his time in Boston, Hari also designed ties, handkerchiefs and scarves carrying the of all religions. He started distributing them to everyone he met.

Hari with Professor Prema Pandurang during her discourse on Srimad Bhagwat Gita at the Kanoria House

Hari addressing an audience in Chicago, 2018

Hari with Swami Swaroopanand Saraswati Maharaj at the World Confluence of Humanity, Power & Spirituality held in 2011

Chapter 56

Reliving the Past

One of Hari Prasad Kanoria's favourite pastimes is to tell his children and grandchildren all about the interesting moments of his life. There is so much love, so much bliss and so much innocence in them that he can't help but go down the memory lane.

Once he went to Iceland with Sunil, his wife Sunita and their children, Anant and Avani. There he rode a motorcycle up an icy mountain His balance was so perfect, not once did he skid. Everyone wondered how it was possible—they knew Hari was against bikes and had never ridden one.

Hari smiled and shared his childhood memories of Barhiya—when seven to eight boys would ride one bicycle! Little did he know that a simple experience from so many decades ago would perfect his balance to such an extent that even in his seventies he would be able to ride a motorcycle without losing control.

Many things remind him of his past—and he gets excited about sharing it with whoever is with him as he believes they may learn something from it.

Whenever he eats curd, he remembers Barhiya—with the cows, and how his grandmother would milk them every morning. In fact, his ever fertile mind has come up with his own recipe for sweet yogurt based on botanical principles and human evolutions. Anyone who comes home, will be force fed the recipe (add jaggery to a table spoon of yogurt) as well as a large bowl of the famous Hari Kanoria 'mishti doi' (sweet curd).

When he faces a bully at work, he is reminded of the one

he faced years ago, in Calcutta, after which he had to hide in a water tank for hours.

He recalls those joyful moments when he carried Mukund, his eldest grandson (son of Dr Sanjeev) on his shoulder (like a villager) while walking on the streets of Birmingham and other places even as by-passers smiled at them in amusement.

When one of his children give him an opportunity to feel proud, he is instantly reminded of his grandfather and father to whom he gave several opportunities to cry happy tears.

He realizes that everything is interconnected and deeply cherishes his past for the present it has brought to him—and the future it promises.

I sometimes feel that Hari Prasad is an inspiring story book. Open any page and you will find something to be happy about, something to fall in love with and something to smile. It's amazing to have lived a life that you can keep referring to with peace and enthusiasm—all in the same breath.

Chapter 57

The Little Guru

There is a saying about grandparents that for them their children are the milk, but their grandchildren are the cream. They can do anything and everything for their grandchildren, and love just seems to be magnified infinite times over.

For Hari, his children were his world, so one can readily imagine what his grandchildren mean to him. And if grandchildren are so dear to him, imagine how he would feel about having a—great grand-daughter in his life?

When Siddhi's daughter Rajveka was born in 2012, and she was a delight for the entire Kanoria family. Whenever she visits the Kanoria home, time seems to stand still for everyone. Everyone literally leaves whatever they are engaged in and start playing with the angelic doll who knows very well the kind of impact her mere presence has on a household full of adults. Most of all, she cherishes her time with her 'Bara Nanu' (Hari, her great grandfather) because she feels they are equals—despite the 70-plus years' gap.

In her presence, Bara Nanu stops all his work and runs around with her. He will laugh with her, he will tickle her, he will pamper her and he will tell her stories of gods and goddesses from heaven as well as those from his own life.

Rajveka, on her part, considers it her personal duty to guide Bara Nanu on the nitty gritty of life. Whenever he does puja, he tries to teach her how to put 'tikka' (saffron) on the photographs/statues of the deities, and since it is done differently in her own house, little Rajveka tells him how it is to be done. She tells him, in a firm way (like a grown-up), 'What Bara Nanu—you have grown so big but you still don't know the little things of life!' Moments like this are beautiful for Hari.

For Bara Nanu, Rajveka's little fingers, her big round eyes, her laughter resounding through the hallway of their home, or her mock shouting at him—all of it is nothing short of manna from heaven. He loves wandering around with her in his arms through the gardens, plucking litchis and mangoes. He absolutely adores his little great granddaughter and waits for every opportunity to be with her.

I had the opportunity of watching the duo several times. It is the cutest of relationships. When Hari Prasad and Rajveka are together, it is difficult to say who is younger or naughtier. The two of them run around the long hallways of the Kanoria home, creating memories worth preserving for a lifetime, with every step.

Great granddaughter Rajveka—the apple of his eye

Chapter 58

Strong Roots, Powerful Wings

Hari Prasad Kanoria believes immensely in the potential of children. He believes that the future of India and the world depends on what we are doing for our youth. He feels that the more we contribute towards a holistic, spiritual and modern education of children, the better tomorrow's generation will be.

Towards this ideal, the Kanorias are actively supporting poor students through the Ramakrishna Mission. In fact, close to eight hundred students are being funded through the Kanoria Foundation. Besides this, Sunita, Sunil's wife, runs the Suryodaya School for underprivileged children where, not just education, but also food and clothes are provided free of cost.

Besides, the Kanorias are running a Montessori school as well as a CBSE-affiliated school with affordable fees catering to around seven hundred students around Kolkata. In 2017, the Kanorias founded a school, the Srihari Global School in Asansol, and the eldest grand-daughter-in-law, Shruti is managing it with a lot of love and passion.

For Hari, children are the seeds which have the potential to become the forests. He blossoms when he sees children grow to their capability and feels excited when someone exhibits extraordinary talent. He is always encouraging youngsters in the family and in his circle of influence to grow strong roots as well as powerful wings, which will help them to deal with the vagaries of life in a befitting and graceful manner.

Hari feels privileged to have had the kind of upbringing and care he received from the elders in his family. They taught him so much about himself, relationships, business, health, wealth and life—and he wishes to do the same for as many as possible, directly and indirectly. His mission is to follow the path of Swami Vivekananda who said, 'Educate people intellectually, technically and morally.'

Hari set up a solar Charkha and loom for spinning yarn as well as weaving looms for weaving fabric at his village, Barhiya, for empowering women to have self employment. More than 400 women have been trained. Over 100 solar charkhas were installed in the houses of 52 women and from their earnings they will pay the installment of solar charkha themselves.

Srihari Global IISD Foundation (formerly IISD Edu World)

Srihari Global School

Chapter 59

The Great Wall of China

When Tom Sawyer saw a wall, he painted it.
When most people see walls, they walk in another direction.

When Hari Prasad Kanoria sees a wall, he climbs it, be it a simple 15-feet wall he climbed as a child or the Great Wall of China. For Hari, walls are made to be climbed.

In 2003, Hari visited China along with the then Prime Minister Atal Bihari Vajpayee and a few select businessmen. Hari's curiosity about everything and wonderment propelled the entire group to go sightseeing, which included a visit to the Great Wall of China. Seeing the age, shape and health of the delegates, Hari did not have the heart to say, 'Come, let's climb the wall!' However, in his mind he decided that one day he would.

Life gave him the opportunity in 2008 when the Bharat Chamber of Commerce took a delegation to China, and Hari was among them. He told the organizers, 'I will only join you if you allow my grandsons to come along with me.' Initially they were a little reluctant, but they knew how much value Hari added to any group—with his jovial nature, intelligent insights and happy-go-lucky attitude, and so they said, 'Sure, Mr Kanoria—bring them along.'

Mukund, Raghav as well as Anant went with their grandfather. Vatsal, Mukund's younger brother was to join them, but at the last moment he had a stomach upset and hence opted out.

There he was, once again, before the Great Wall of China. None of the other delegates (much younger than Hari) expressed the slightest interest or inclination to climb it, so Hari decided to do it on his own. His grandsons, seeing their grandfather's enthusiasm, joined him. Finally, he was there—on top, where he liked to be.

Hari accomplished many other 'firsts' as well while he was in China. He remembers that trip with a lot of love and fondness. His children and grandchildren are his world, and quality time invested in them. It was also the country where he first ate pasta, spaghetti and Chinese dishes.

There was a certain place where his grandsons wanted to have pizza. The delegates refused to stop, saying that lunch had already been fixed elsewhere. Hari replied, 'No problem, we will get down and take another cab! You all carry on, I cannot deny my grandchildren this treat!'

Seeing his love for his grandchildren, and possibly being tempted by the company as well as the pizza, all the delegates decided to take a detour and stop at the restaurant. It was a lunch they would always remember as it was filled with lots of laughter, interesting conversations and pizzas that were worth the detour.

I just love the way Hari Prasad's eyes light up when he is talking about his children or grandchildren. There is this aura of tenderness, protective love and bliss around him each time he talks about them. Blessed are the Kanoria youngsters who have a grandfather who dotes on them like this. They are, as he keeps saying, his world.

Hari riding a horse at the Great Wall of China

Chapter 60

Giving Back

Hari wanted to create a foundation which would take care of all his children, their wives and grandchildren for years to come. He wanted some unique terms and clauses which seemed to challenge the conventional wisdom of lawyers. Not so to Hari. And as he spoke with conviction to the team which helped him formulate the framework of the family constitution, they realized that even though several clauses seemed ridiculous and unworkable in some way or the other, Hari, along with his eldest son Hemant, would make it happen. The lawyers said to him, 'Since it is you, we will not even attempt to discourage you. We know you will make the impossible happen.'

The foundation takes utmost care of women. It goes to show Hari's love and care for them. Not only has he ensured that his daughter has a fair stake in the family constitution, he has also made elaborate arrangements for each of his daughter-in-law—to the extent that he has even added a clause that in the unfortunate instance that his son and daughter-in-law opt for a divorce, she will be taken care of by the Kanorias until she marries someone else. She will be given the option of taking the children with her, or allowing them to be raised by the Kanoria family. Hari's vision went so far ahead as to include situations that most people won't even dream of.

The foundation does charity work. Hari Prasad Kanoria believes it is their duty to serve those who are less privileged, and a fair share of the foundation's earnings are earmarked for NGOs that work with children and the elderly.

Hari's thought process is simple: I have been given so I can give. What I do is not just for the self, it is for society, and we owe it to the world.

The logo of the Kanoria Foundation depicts the Samudra Manthan, an episode from the Bhagavata Purana, which signifies the churning of the oceans to produce the nectar of immortality. The motto of the Foundation complements the logo: Work With Devotion. It sums up Hari's motto in life.

The family with President Pranab Mukherji

Tha family with great granddaughter Rajveka

Chapter 61

The Survivors

This is yet another initiative of the Kanoria Foundation. The idea started with a meeting held in 2007, comprising doctors, surgeons, professionals, Rotarians, activists and philanthropists, chaired by Hari and addressed by Col Paul Pettigrew, trustee of the Acid Survivors Trust International (ASTI) based in the United Kingdom. He made a strong case for setting up a foundation for acid survivors in India along the lines of ASTI.

After a long gestation and many hiccups, a skeleton organization was finally set up in 2010. Since then, it has traversed a long and difficult journey led by Rahul Verma (who is virtually Hari Prasad Kanoria's right-hand man). Not only is he capable of leading a team on such a sensitive issue, he is also well-versed with the problems of acid survivors. Under his able guidance, the organization is slowly expanding its wings. Centres have been set up in Mumbai, Delhi, Chennai, Patna, Meerut, Prayagraj and Bhubaneswar.

Hari, with his usual enthusiasm and generosity, has extended full support to the cause of acid survivors. He makes it a point to attend as many meetings as possible, dispenses funds without delay towards care-giving for victims, supports livelihood and also boosts the morale of the acid survivors by meeting them and speaking to them about letting go of the past, and looking forward to a better future.

The ASWWF has now attained a good standing. Both Hari and Rahul are hopeful that the organization will grow so much in its reach and vibrancy that it will be able to create awareness, help in prevention and extend support to those who most need it.

A beacon of hope for acid survivors

With Dr Badrinath, founder of Shankar Netralaya

Chapter 62

The Power of Faith

Hari Prasad Kanoria has been to almost every part of the world. From the coldest to the warmest, in his capacity as a father, grandfather, businessman and delegate; to give awards, to receive awards. And yet the aspect of his journeys has been the realization of just how much his heart is in India. And, just how much of an Indian he is.

He knows that at present the situation and condition of India is not good. However, he has this unshakable faith that there will be many adventurous people, with the immense strength of spirituality, who will rise from across the country and take it forward in its journey to becoming a superpower.

Swami Vivekananda claimed in 1897 that India would be independent in fifty years. This did come true—India gained its independence in 1947. Likewise, Hari believes that in a few years India will awaken to its spiritual powers and conquer the world with love, spirituality and values.

Hari, quoting Swami Vivekananda, has written in one of his editorials—India is a sleeping dragon. The day it rises to take its rightful place as a spiritual as well as an economic powerhouse, no power will be able to stop it.

Whenever Hari speaks of India, his voice becomes emotional, his eyes get moist and he speaks almost as if India is a person—with whom he has the most intimate of all relationships—not a geographical location or a spot on the map.

There is immense power in faith. The more I have come in contact with Hari Prasad Kanoria, the more I have realized that everything he is, is all about faith in self, and faith in God. Usually, when someone talks about India, I am always a little sceptical. But I am very optimistic about the future of this great country when someone like Hari speaks. It re-iterates my belief in India.

At the inaugural session of the Calcutta Chamber of Commerce

With the then President A.P.J. Abdul Kalam

Chapter 63

The Spiritual Confluence

It was in 2009 that the germ of an idea was born in Hari's mind. Inspired by Swami Vivekananda and his life's mission to selflessly, righteously and fearlessly take India towards a spiritual uprising for harmony and happiness, Hari came up with the idea of starting an annual event—a world confluence of humanity, power and spirituality at a global level—where different religious leaders, politicians, bureaucrats, professionals, industrialists, businessmen and youth would interact with one another to take the cause to another level.

The first meeting was held at the Calcutta Club. Hari, Rahul, Nishi (from the SREI team) and Manisha met to discuss the vision, execution and feasibility of a confluence like this. The idea was to create a mega event to draw global attention—something at a very large scale to represent the spirit of India and its spiritual roots.

Hari was deeply inspired by the thoughts of oneness. He wanted to create a platform for people from various religions, across gender, age, countries and cultures, to share their views on how the world could rise above narrow definitions and limited worldviews. How could we free the world to embrace a culture of deep love, respect and understanding, and create a sense of unity among diversity?

A lot of thoughts were put together within this immediate group—and then gradually these thoughts were taken to different groups across the globe. It seemed to be an idea whose time had come. Many others were waiting for an opportunity like this, to bring the forces together and do good work. They were only too willing to participate.

What began as a thought, culminated in the first ever World Confluence of Humanity, Power and Spiritual Enlightenment, in Kolkata, where forty delegates representing different streams came together to share their concerns and take the movement forward.

The event has grown so much in popularity and prominence in the last few years that it has had speakers from across the globe including famous politicians, sages, doctors, lawyers, philanthropists and influencers. From H.H. Dwarka—Jotishpeethadhapati Jagatguru Shankaracharya Swami Swaroopanand Saraswati Maharaj and the princess of Philippines to the head of the Ajmer Sharif Dargah, from former presidents of India, A.P.J. Abdul Kalam and Pranab Mukherjee to the founder of infinitheism, Mahatria, and Jaggi Vasudev of Isha Foundation, and actor Vivek Oberoi—eminent personalities have been a part of this wonderful confluence.

The then President Pranab Mukherjee lighting the lamp

THE SPIRITUAL CONFLUENCE • 157

The Spiritual Confluence

The multi-faith Spiritual Confluence

With the then President Pratibha Patil

With the then Vice President Bhairon Singh Shekhawat

THE SPIRITUAL CONFLUENCE • 159

With Mahatria Ra

A quiet moment with Sadhguru

With Sri Sri Ravi Shankar

With the then President Pranab Mukherjee

With Sister Shivani and B.K. Kanan

Dr H.P. Kanoria with Dr Ellen Baker, former NASA astronaut

Vedant as Vivekanand

Vatsal and Yagesh

THE SPIRITUAL CONFLUENCE • 163

World Confluence of Humanity, Power & Spirituality

2010 - 2015

A collage of World Confluence of Humanity, Power & Spirituality 2016-2019

Chapter 64

My Friend Kalam

Over the years, Hari has made many friends. Some are close friends with whom he has a 'dinner', 'chai' and 'chat' relationship. Some are eminent personalities with whom he discusses the future of the world. Some are top politicians with whom Hari has a personal as well as professional understanding. There are spiritualists with whom Hari experiences the delights of the soul. And there are celebrities, who seek him for patronage!

There is no dearth of inspiring presences in the life of Hari. And they claim when they meet him, something about their life opens up in ways they cannot comprehend.

Hari Prasad was also awarded a doctorate in Literature by Master Meher Moos. Around the same time, a special friendship blossomed between Hari and former president Dr A.P.J. Kalam.

In 2004, Hari was the president of the Agri-Horticultural Society of India, established in 1820, and having a large area of twenty-five acres with a variety of plants in the heart of Kolkata. Hari developed the 'herbal block' there and even wrote a book called *Herbal Power*. He went to invite the then president, A.P.J. Abdul Kalam, to inaugurate the herbal block. The two had an engaging discussion about plants. After the discussion, the president asked Hari, 'Are you a horticulturist?' Hari answered, 'I am a small businessman.' Hari also presented his periodical magazine *Business Economics* and gifted him a couple of plants grown at the Society. Kalam agreed to inaugurate the herbal block as he liked the genuineness he saw in Hari.

The president arrived in Kolkata and inaugurated the herbal

block. After the inauguration, he was scheduled to address the gathering of the society, which also included many youngsters. The security officials accompanying the president insisted that he go by car from the herbal block to the dais, which was some distance away. When the president saw that Hari was walking to the place where the stage had been erected, he got down from the car and started walking with him. Such was the humility of President Kalam.

Inspired by the work done by the Society, President Kalam also decided to build a herbal block and enlightenment block in Rashtrapati Bhavan.

Hari and President Kalam met several times after that. They became close friends, and, in 2007, when Dr Kalam relinquished the office of the president of India and moved to his official residence, Hari gifted him with hundreds of plants so that he would not miss the beauty of the gardens he had enjoyed in the Rashtrapati Bhavan.

Dr Kalam also launched Hari's book, *Enlightenment*, during the 4th World Confluence of Humanity, Power and Spirituality, in 2012. He also graced and addressed the Confluence.

None other than Dr Kalam blessed Manisha's wonderful initiative called iSpark, a holistic growth centre for health and happiness in Chennai, which also has its own e-magazine, *iSpark: Aspire to Inspire*, created to encourage a spirit of enquiry and wonderment about the self, others and life in children.

One has many friends in life. And yet, some continue to linger on, and on irrespective of their physical presence. For Hari, Dr Kalam will always remain one such friend. Someone poignantly wrote upon his demise—'India, divided by states, communal feeling and religious sentiments—united by one man—Dr Kalam.'

With A.P.J. Abdul Kalam

With Hemant and A.P.J. Abdul Kalam

Chapter 65

A Child at Heart

Age does not seem to have touched Hari at all. His beaming countenance, child-like laughter and enthusiasm for anything and everything in life is very endearing, and touches the heart.

What keeps him so ageless?

Hari Prasad Kanoria believes it has a lot to do with his zest for life. He is unstoppable when it comes to drinking in the beauty of new experiences. We age when we feel each day is just like the other. For Hari, this simply didn't exist. He believes firmly in the saying, 'You can never step into the same river twice…' which signifies that everything about life is in such a state of flux that everything is renewed every nanosecond.

Hari recalls the time he went on an Alaskan cruise with Sunil, Sunita, Anant and Avani. Although Hari had experienced a snowfall on numerous points in time in his life, his heart was filled with delight when he experienced the soft white showers during their trip, as though it was the very first time.

Much to the amusement of his son, daughter-in-law and grandchildren, he climbed an icy hill and began sliding down the icy slope like a child, laughing like there was nothing else that mattered. His entire face had lit up, his eyes were shining like never before and 'Wheeeeee' he went, just like babies would, tumbling, toppling and rolling, even though he was well into his seventies!

There were helicopter rides between mountains, and he insisted that he wanted to do everything there was to do. Even though the others weren't that excited about it, his enthusiasm—

contagious that it was—rubbed off on them and soon the entire family was ready to experience things they hadn't before.

Hari has beautiful memories to share about each of his grandchildren. Be it the provision-shopping experience with Vedant, the chocolate binging with Yagyesh in Boston, or being in Nicco Park with Vatsal, the stories abound!

In 2015, the family visited the Andaman Islands where scuba diving was being taught. Hari was the first to raise his hand when asked who wanted to join in. The grandsons told Hari, 'It might be risky, Dadu.' However, Sanjeev encouraged him and said, 'Go for it, Papa!'

Hari did.

It was an inexplicable feeling—to be in the blue water, along with so many shiny, colourful fish. He felt it was a spiritual experience to become one with the water and discover a land of mystical creatures.

Once he re-surfaced, he thought to himself, *Always say yes to every new experience; you never know what you will miss out on, if you don't!*

Whenever I have seen Hari Prasad—in the middle of a Confluence with hundreds of people, or all alone; at 5 in the morning or at midnight; doing yoga or walking at Victoria Gardens; at his office or in the comforts of the large massage chair which dominates his bedroom—if there is one expression that never seems to leave him, it is that of a little one. There is such a sense of wonder in his eyes, such a yearning for 'something more' that whenever I am with him—something magical happens to me as well. I feel ageless, timeless. Just suspended in the moment, making the most of it.

Hari scuba diving

Always game to try something new

Chapter 66

Paradox No More

The person who began writing this book, sometime in January 2018, and the person who finished it on 4 July 2019, is not the same. Over the last one-and-a-half years, so much has happened—for Hari Prasad and for me.

The last time I met him, he was attending the convocation ceremony of his daughter Manisha, who was being given the title of 'doctor' in Mumbai for her significant social contribution. He was smiling from ear to ear—like he usually does.

When you see him with his majestic persona, sitting on any chair, making it look like a throne, you might not know about his journey—from a village like Barhiya, to having a business in almost every country; from being the little boy who hid inside a water tank to protect himself to becoming the founder of a company where more than 10,000 people wait for a single gesture from him to do what they must; from freely roaming through the lanes of Barhiya to winning so many prestigious awards, including the 'Global Man of the Year 2015' at the 3rd Annual Global Officials of Dignity (G.O.D.) Awards, held in August 2015, at the United Nations headquarters in New York. This is highest recognition conferred to an individual for exemplary contributions to humanity.

The best part is, when you see Hari Prasad, running around with Rajveka or reading a newspaper looking for some new opportunity; hollering at the cook for what he wants to eat or walking around at the horticulture garden, you do not see an eighty-year-old reminiscing over a life spectacularly led. Rather, you see a curious teen, rubbing his hands together in wonderment, thinking—what more, what next, what more, what next...

In Hari, I found a man who makes the balancing of various paradoxes of life look as effortless as walking barefoot in the grass. From making crucial business decisions to cracking a joke with a grandchild; from being a playful husband to a powerful industrialist; from having a listed business growing in the material realms to seeking spiritual solace among enlightened souls—his life is such a beautiful mix of paradoxes.

From him I have learnt the six key attributes towards greatness; from him I have learnt to think win/win, no matter what life says to you. His child-like enthusiasm too seems to have kindled the same in me, which may have been dormant for a while. I find myself humming through work, I find myself whistling through challenges and dancing through several situations in my life which would earlier have caused a different reaction. I feel altered in ways I can understand, and in many ways which only the future will reveal. I hope the book does the same for you.

There is a beautiful phrase in Buddhism, called *Charaiveti, Charaiveti*—which means keep going. This is the end of the book. But I believe it is the beginning of yet another phase in Hari Prasad Kanoria's life (and mine). I am excited to see what is coming. *Charaiveti, Charaiveti...*

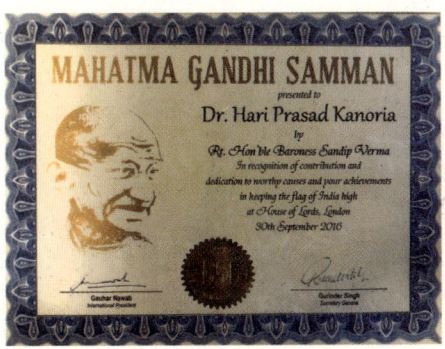

The award presented at the House of Lords, London

Master blaster Sachin Tendulkar presenting an award to Dr Kanoria

Being felicitated at the Nehru Centre, London

Hari Prasad Kanoria being presented the Global Man of the Year Award by US Senator, Diane Watson, at the 3rd Annual God Awards at the United Nations, New York, in August 2015. The Global Officials of Dignity (G.O.D.) Award was in recognition of Dr Kanoria's outstanding and invaluable services to the community.

Shri Kedarnath Kanoria with Shri Krishna Sinha,
the then chief minister of Bihar

From left to right—Shri Jyoti Basu, the then chief minister of West Wengal
with N.K. Jalan, Hari and S.S. Swaika

Hari with Shri Somnath Chatterjee, former Speaker of Lok Sabha

I.C. Sancheti, Lokenath Dokania, Hari, B.S. Shekhawat (the then Vice President of India), N.K. Jalan, Sitaram Sharma, Ratan Saha and Pawan Jalan

Hari with daughter-in-law Sangita Kanoria and the then president Dr A.P.J. Abdul Kalam at the Rashtrapati Bhavan

Hari and Champa's 50th wedding anniversary

Hari Prasad Kanoria with his great granddaughter Rajveka

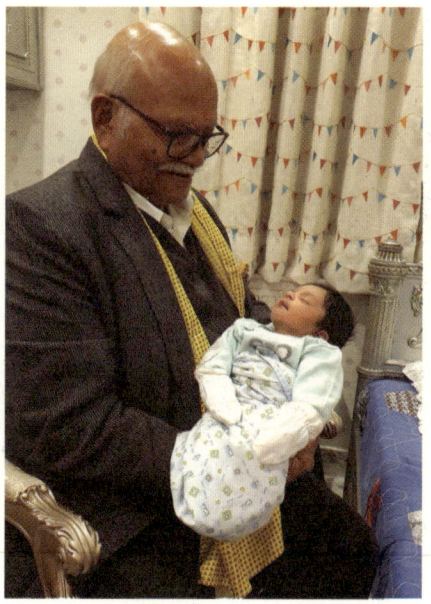

Hari with his great granddaughter Pranavi

Dr Kanoria, Manisha Lohia and Megha Bajaj during the making of the book.

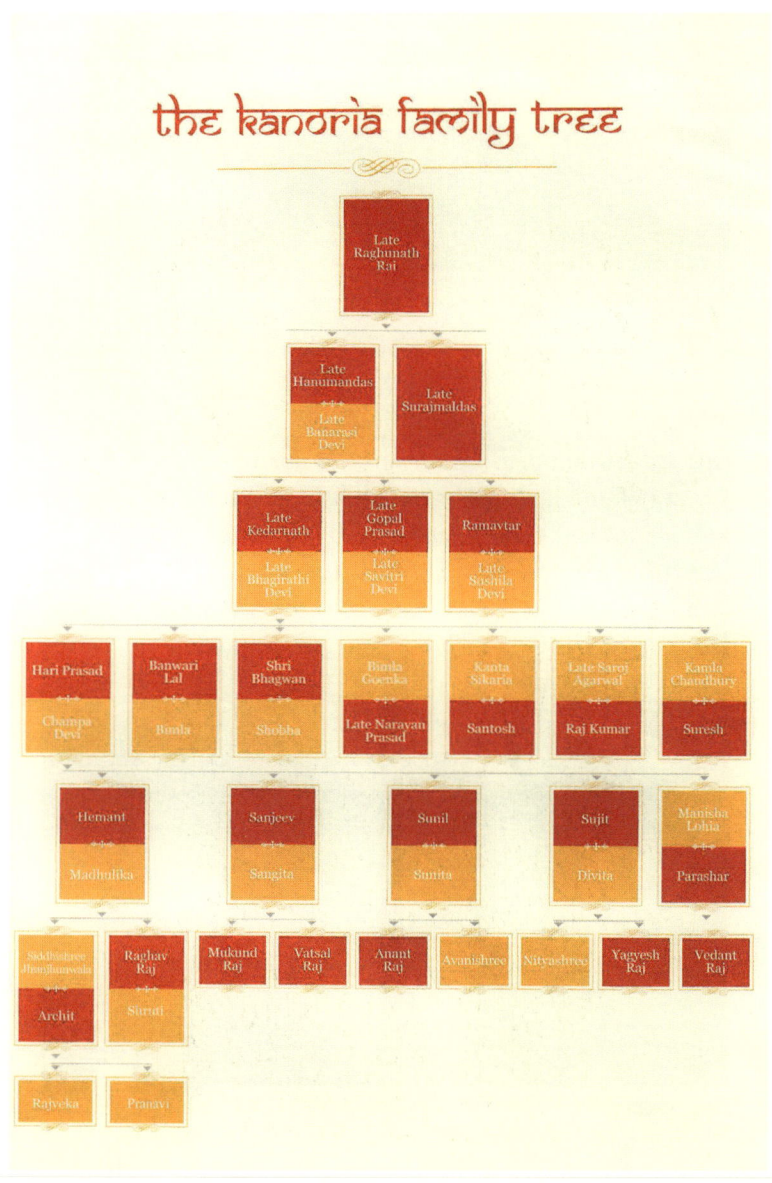

God has manifested the universe by his thoughts and will. We are manifested in His image. We are immortal, perfect, infinite, divine. God is seated in the heart of all. The soul, which is immortal does not have any gender.

Connect to God's will. Surrender our will at the altar of His will. Say utterly in love, 'Thy will be done.'

—Dr H.P. Kanoria
(An explanation of the messages of
Swami Vivekananda and other scriptures.)